T0368478

Copyright © 2018 by Marcus Westnedge. 743744
Library of Congress Control Number: 2016916655

ISBN: Softcover   978-1-5245-1814-1
        Hardcover   978-1-5245-1815-8
        EBook   978-1-5245-1813-4

All rights reserved. No part of this book may
be reproduced or transmitted in any form or by
any means, electronic or mechanical, including
photocopying, recording, or by any information storage
and retrieval system, without permission in writing from
the copyright owner.

Print information available on the last page

Rev. date: 04/11/2018

To order additional copies of this book, contact:
Xlibris
1-800-455-039
www.xlibris.com.au
Orders@Xlibris.com.au

Homes for Heroes – Help for Vets in Need

Thank you. You're helping transform homeless ex-service families' lives.

By buying this book, you're helping young ex-service people and their families' move from homelessness back into civilian life.

Shamefully, there are over 3,000 men and women who defended your and my home, only to face into homelessness in the challenging transition from discharge to civilian life. We want to change this.

We aim to be a part of the solution by giving 100% of the proceeds of the sale of this book to Narrabeen RSL LifeCare and their incredible Homes for Heroes program (rsllifecare.org.au/young-veterans).

You've just joined the Capital Properties' mission to fulfil an important calling.

Can you even imagine what it's like to have no home? Sadly, homeless war veterans are getting younger and younger.

The Homes for Heroes program is getting young Australian war veterans back on the road to recovery from post traumatic stress disorder. The Program is achieving this by providing accommodation options and a whole range of support services to help homeless ex-service people return from living off the streets, back into society.

Congratulations. You've just got personally involved in a cause which touches all members of the Australian Defence Force – current and past. Your payment for this book will help fund much needed special support programs and service to help ease the shift from discharge, to civvy street.

You can help raise awareness and transform lives for the better.

Please help raise awareness by jumping onto your favourite social media and tagging:

I support #Homes4Heroes http://rsllifecare.org.au/young-veterans/

Hop onto Facebook and 'Like' and then 'Share' the Facebook page and ask friends to do the same:

https://www.facebook.com/homelessvetsoz/

Help is at hand if you need it right now.

If you're in an emergency situation, please call Homes for Heroes on 0408 928 432 right now.

Thank you endlessly.

We would like to take this opportunity to acknowledge the strength, courage and dedication of all our Australian service men and women in defending our homes. Thank you. Thank you. Thank you.

We'd love to hear what you thought of this book. Drop us an email.

We hope reading this book has inspired you to take action. We're good listeners and always looking for ways to improve. Your feedback would be a huge help in helping us, help others. Please write to info@ capitalproperties.com.au with the subject line: Property Investment SOPs Book Review.

Kindest regards from all of the Capital Properties' team.

PROPERTY INVESTMENT STANDARD OPERATING PROCEDURE (SOP)

BEGINNERS GUIDE

PROPERTY INVESTMENT

FOR SWITCHED-ON PEOPLE

THE QUICK GUIDE FOR THE DEFENCE FORCE PROPERTY INVESTOR

DEVELOP A STRATEGY TO ACHIEVE YOUR LIFESTYLE
GOALS WHILE SERVING IN THE MILITARY

Acknowledgements

Firstly, a massive thank you Mum and Dad. You guys were the ones who steered me on this path and without your nagging (Mum) I wouldn't have got my first deposit saved and first deal done. Imagine if all parents did this! You guys are champions and have always been so supportive. THANK YOU.

There are many others, who without even knowing it inspired me with your words of encouragement, bold actions, and character traits to mimic. Without help we are on our own, and therefore limited to what we can do by ourselves. Success is a combined effort! Not one successful person ever got there by themselves.

There are too many people to thank on one page. Most of you I know personally but some I don't. All of you have made a tremendous impact on my personal journey in more ways than you can imagine – THANK YOU!

What others are saying about this book

As a Senior Sailor, finding time to read outside of Defence responsibilities can be challenging. With an easy to follow format, clearly defined steps and relatable stories that help break down otherwise complicated investment concepts, Capital Properties Standard Operating Procedure was a welcome read. Aimed at peers beginning to look at investing, the material was equally valuable to experienced investors. With lifestyle goals driving your investment strategy, this guide redefines the objectives of property investment. Marcus sets tasks that challenge your intent and focus on taking action task by task, rather than just thinking about investing. The SOP steps you through the journey from strategy development to analysing cash flow to reviewing the performance of your investment properties. This is a well written resource and one I intend to reference in the future.

Daniel J., Senior Sailor R.A.N.

Marcus has pulled together an easy and practical guide on how to face the fear of committing to property investment head on, while balancing the demands of our busy (and social) Defence lifestyles. From the outset, it's clear that he gets it and that the book has been written especially for members of Defence. While a simple read, it is energising because it puts the spotlight on the financial control that we all hold in every direct deposit of pay into our bank accounts. This read is a great starting point in that it provides you with the initial tools you need to get started in property investment. I'd highly recommend - Property Investment SOP to any Defence member thinking about how to start channelling their income into property investment to set them up for the future, while still enjoying living a balanced life.

– Mark S. Commanding Officer R.A.N

In working through the book, you can tell Marcus knows from personal experience that property investing takes work and commitment. His manual commands that you put pen to paper (or finger to keypad) as you work through practical steps - setting it apart from other investment guides. Marcus shares his own personal story of starting and building a property investment folio as a young Navy officer. He's been there, and he gets the Defence life, making for a relatable guide for young Defence Force members ready to carve out their future. As a civilian I found this SOP highly relevant. The author demystifies property investment terminology by applying it to real life property purchase calculations. I found this particularly helpful. At the same time, his casual, friendly tone throughout the book makes you feel like you've got a friend backing you. Marcus' passion for the opportunities property can open up shines through. For those keen to deconstruct the 'why' behind property investing, or for those ready to make property work for them, this manual will be your 'go to' for years to come.

– Julie Pearce, Editor Content Services Melbourne

Forward

When I was writing this book, I wanted to run alongside of a centralised theme which is entwined in the fabric of this guide.

All the content leads back to this central question – 'How can I help unleash a set of ideas that shapes the future of our Defence Force members' financial life that impacts the sense of what's possible to achieve their important goals, in line with their lifestyle and current financial position?'

It's a bit of a mouth full I know! Everything leads back to this and my hope is that what you learn from working through this book helps you make the most of this opportunity you have in your hands today to encourage you to dream bigger.

My hope is that this book assists you to create the type of life you want and are striving towards.

Table of Contents

AUTHORITY FOR ISSUE

This Standard Operating Procedure (SOP) is issued under the guidance of Capital Properties – a friendly, knowledgeable bunch of trusted residential property experts and licensed estate agents. Capital Properties actively encourages readers of this SOP to learn and grow, starting now.

Congratulations on taking the first important step toward your secure financial future.

www.capitalproperties.com.au

Marcus Westnedge

Founder and Director of Capital Properties Pty Ltd

(Ex Royal Australian Navy)

www.capitalproperties.com.au

PART 1

Switched-on property investment and 'the why'

Quite simply, I want you equipped to set yourself up for a future full of choices while you're young.

The nomadic Defence lifestyle can mean coming home cashed up, and tempted to spend up big. Too often I saw ship-mates let opportunities pass them by at a time when their lives were less complicated. Making sure *you* get off to a great start is my motivation for sharing this guide.

You may not see it clearly now, but you're already winning in life.

You have a steady income and a pay scale to climb if you want to. If you grab the advantages in front of you early and master saving a portion of that income, you can set yourself up for life.

I've been where you are. I know what works best for the lifestyle you lead.

THE SECRET TO ACHIEVING WEALTH IS EDUCATION

Some education on how to set goals, save some cash and invest in the right property can see you on your way to setting up a passive income.

In this guide, I'll share an investment strategy tailored for your Defence lifestyle. It's a strategy that works best for busy Defence people that enjoy their job while they invest in long term goals.

I'm sharing my story to show you what is possible. I served this country for twelve years. I know what it feels like to go on lengthy deployments while wanting to get ahead in life.

I grew my property investment portfolio while embracing the challenges of a Navy career. In my spare time, I grew a property portfolio. I still had a great time with my mates, but I also knew where I was heading.

> "I believe that education is the key to unlocking those hidden paths tied to the achievement of one's goals."
> – Marcus Westnedge

Today, those early decisions allow me to surf when I want to, live where I want to and work when I want to.

Most people want to do well in life. Knowing how to bridge the gap of where they are right now ('A') and where they want to get to – their future goals ('B'), is the biggest challenge. The most effective vehicle to guide you from A to B is education.

Ignorance is far more costly than education. Today, education is more accessible than ever before.

For being proactive in educating yourself on property investing, I'm going to walk you through a seven step process in this guide. Own it!

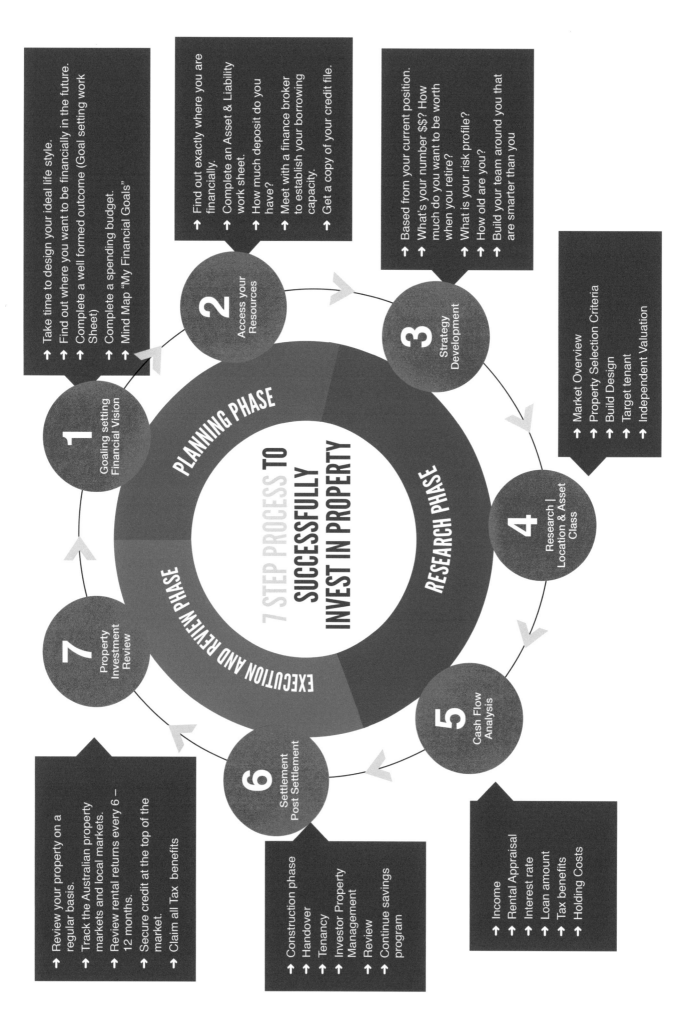

7 STEP PROCESS TO SUCCESSFULLY INVEST IN PROPERTY

PLANNING PHASE

RESEARCH PHASE

EXECUTION AND REVIEW PHASE

1 Goaling setting Financial Vision
- Take time to design your ideal life style.
- Find out where you want to be financially in the future.
- Complete a well formed outcome (Goal setting work Sheet)
- Complete a spending budget.
- Mind Map "My Financial Goals"

2 Access your Resources
- Find out exactly where you are financially.
- Complete an Asset & Liability work sheet.
- How much deposit do you have?
- Meet with a finance broker to establish your borrowing capacity.
- Get a copy of your credit file.

3 Strategy Development
- Based from your current position.
- What's your number $$? How much do you want to be worth when you retire?
- What is your risk profile?
- How old are you?
- Build your team around you that are smarter than you

4 Research | Location & Asset Class
- Market Overview
- Property Selection Criteria
- Build Design
- Target tenant
- Independent Valuation

5 Cash Flow Analysis
- Income
- Rental Appraisal
- Interest rate
- Loan amount
- Tax benefits
- Holding Costs

6 Settlement Post Settlement
- Construction phase
- Handover
- Tenancy
- Investor Property Management
- Review
- Continue savings program

7 Property Investment Review
- Review your property on a regular basis.
- Track the Australian property markets and local markets.
- Review rental returns every 6 – 12 months.
- Secure credit at the top of the market.
- Claim all Tax benefits

About this Quick Start Edition

This booklet is a quick start property investing guide personalised for Defence people.

This is not a get-rich-quick-scheme. There is no such scheme. Wealth building is a long term process.

You're about to kick off that process by learning some basics on how and where to get started in property investing – lessons straight from my life experiences.

This Quick Start Edition is a general guide designed to be straightforward and achievable.

With the basics under your shoulder patch, you can continue to build your knowledge. Property investment is a lifelong learning adventure. I've never stopped learning.

As you work through each of the steps, you'll feel a greater sense of control of your finances.

I hope you'll find it an enjoyable process and that in turn, you can pass on knowledge to others. Switched-on property investors inspire those around them, leaving a legacy of knowledge and assets for future generations.

A 7 step SOP to successfully reach your future goals

The diagram on brings the 7 step framework together in one snapshot.

Let's break down the framework that will guide your decisions to set you up for the future you want, starting today. You need to:

1. SET FINANCIAL GOALS TO SUPPORT YOUR LIFESTYLE GOALS

If you use GPS to set your destination to get there via the most efficient route, why wouldn't you apply the same principle to life? Simply by defining your goals and writing or typing them down, you'll position yourself to earn 9 times more in your lifetime than your mate that has no idea of their destination.

2. UNDERSTAND YOUR FINANCIAL POSITION TO ACCESS RESOURCES TO INVEST

Once you know where you're going, you need to understand your financial position today so you can work out what financial resources you can access to achieve your goals. To borrow for an investment property, your financial records will need to be ship shape. Then it's off to a finance broker to find out what your borrowing power is.

> "If you want to live a happy life, tie it to a goal, not to people or things."
> – Albert Einstein

3. BUILD YOUR STRATEGY BY PUTTING A TEAM OF EXPERTS AROUND YOU

Your financial goals won't be the same as your mate's. This is why a one size fits all strategy is a myth. Once you've got your goals and where you are now down, it's time to get a team around you that can offer expert guidance on how to bridge the gap to achieve success.

> "If you're the smartest person in your team, find a new team! This applies to me too!"
> – Marcus Westnedge

4. MAKE STRATEGY DRIVEN DECISIONS BACKED BY PROVEN RESEARCH CRITERIA

Proven property investment research criteria will help you choose the right property. Start with a nationwide, capital city view of the Australian property markets, then narrow it down based on detailed location criteria. It's a zoom out, zoom in approach. Once you've targeted a local area, you need to research what type of asset best fits your strategy. When you're young, your focus is towards growth.

5. UNDERSTAND CASH FLOW ANALYSIS TO SUCCEED IN PROPERTY INVESTMENT

The zoom out, zoom in location criteria for choosing property are two of three key investment principles. The third is cash flow analysis - a great skill to tuck under your Defence cap. Practiced enough, you'll know exactly where you're sitting in terms of your cash flow, and how an addition to your portfolio might take you toward your goals.

6. GET EDUCATED ON PRE-SETTLEMENT AND POST-SETTLEMENT MILESTONES

In the process of buying investment property, you need to achieve some key milestones before and after the settlement takes place. By educating yourself before you buy your investment property you'll avoid costly risks like attracting penalty interest and facing longer construction times. You want to reduce your exposure to risk – always – by shortening the time frame from handover to tenancy.

7. REVIEW YOUR PROPERTY INVESTMENT

With good planning based on expert advice, property investing is a set-and-forget strategy - but that doesn't mean you forget about it completely! Property markets shift. Economic conditions shift. You need to be ready to shift too. Regular review of your cash flow position, the property market, the rental market and taxation changes are essential to maximise the return on your switched-on investment strategy.

Having an expert team of property professionals around you will streamline this SOP. For example, keeping a simple but detailed property investment spreadsheet at the ready for your accountant will give you a clear sense of where you're at on your road trip toward your destination.

YOUR NEXT STEP STARTS TODAY

I'm confident you'll get a lot out of your investment of time in reading this guide.

Set aside a good, focused block of time to indulge in building a plan for your future.

Grab a pen and a piece of paper – or if you're an app fanatic, open your favourite note organisation app – and get ready to make loads of notes. Use the tools and resources in this guide to help map out your personalised plan.

This guide is just for you, so you can scribble away like a switched-on property investor.

If you want to continue to work through this guide at your own pace but keen to get started in property investing now, book in to our free, personalised Discovery Session. Just complete the registration form at capitalproperties.com.au > Learn & Grow > Free Discovery Session and fast track your path to successful investing.

Practice your way to success: are you ready?

You'll need to start out with some theory.

Think of this as the start of your new apprenticeship. Once you've got the theory down, you can get practical. Through buying an investment property, you'll reinforce your learnings. By repeating this process over a period of years you'll sharpen your skills and master your trade.

Starting anything new can feel overwhelming. Hang in there. I know the outcomes of this campaign you've volunteered for. Let me be your oppo through this. I'll give you some good structure and guidance based on what I've learnt.

Who would have thought a guy who failed high school and scraped through into the Navy, could put together a seven property, multi-million dollar portfolio by the age of thirty? If I can do this, you can too.

Live life fully. Give this everything you've got. It's worth it, and it does get easier.

Let's shift gears, and talk about fear. It can stop us dead in our tracks. I know. I've been there, conquered it.

How to tackle the fear

Fear is an action killing hurdle that we wire into our brain through past experience and future perceptions of what may or may not be real. When it comes to property investment, fear stems from the unknown.

Knowledge through education will help conquer this fear. Getting clarity on how to cross the bridge toward your future ambitions removes the unknown. All that's missing is a plan. You're already on that bridge by reading this!

Congrats for taking action. Let's go!

I hope you make the most of the opportunity in front of you right now. Enjoy working through your most important SOP yet.

Once you've worked through this guide, I strongly encourage you to take the next step to a rewarding career in property investing.

Here's to your future. See it big, keep it bright, and enjoy the journey.

With very best wishes toward your financial success,

Marcus Westnedge

> "If you want to succeed in property investment, make it your trade." JP – A wise property investor mentor, many years ago.

> Investment n. Expending money with the expectation of achieving a profit or material result by putting it into financial schemes, shares, or property or, devoting (one's time, effort, or energy) to a particular undertaking with the expectation of a worthwhile result.
> - Wikipedia

PART 2

PART 2

Pivotal points shaped my wealth building story

Just 20 years old and a few years in to my Navy career, I bought my first investment property. I didn't understand 'the why' behind the purchase or how it would turn out financially. That decision, and the moments that led up to it were pivotal points that changed my path and transformed my life.

> "The essence of success is the ability to see your vision grow beyond what is was before"
> – Marcus Westnedge.

When I fast forward to today, I am so glad I followed the encouragement and lead of my parents – my first investment mentors - because it was the start of something truly great! I've learned a lot since then and I'm passionate about passing the learning legacy on.

When I reflect on the last 15 years, I can't believe where I've got to. My personal sense of what is possible has shifted up three or four gears from when I was 20!

Feeling pumped about the future with the belief that opportunity is always just around the corner is empowering.

> "Two roads diverged in a wood and I took the one less travelled by, and that has made all the difference."
> – Robert Frost, Poet.

But it didn't start out that way for me. You too will find that your current frame of reference will evolve. As you merge from your familiar surroundings on to the freeway of property investment, your thinking will expand.

A pivotal point is usually a fleeting moment, and yet can change your life. In the moment it can feel like every atom in your body is ready because this is what you're meant to be doing. I've needed to pinch myself occasionally just to make sure where I've got to isn't just a dream!

What is your most pivotal moment so far? I hope reading this guide becomes a pivotal point for you.

JOINING THE NAVY TRANSFORMED MY LIFE (ALONG WITH A PERSISTENT MENTOR!)

I had no idea what I wanted to do with my life when I was 17. I was repeating Year 11 – with my *younger* brother. I wanted out of school. I was trying to get an apprenticeship.

Then it came - a call to join the Navy. I grabbed the opportunity wholeheartedly. This was a pivotal point. I didn't realise it at the time. There are only a handful of decisions in my life that I would call pivotal, but a handful of choices is all it takes. This decision irreversibly changed my life forever.

I've learnt that every minute, every action, every thought and every small decision matters. From my experiences, it's the sequence of smaller events that lines us up for big life moments.

Once I finished recruit school, I made the decision to do category training to become a Marine Technician and later a Clearance Diver. The sequence of these decisions gifted me a secure job with a steady income – a fundamental property investment principle.

Meanwhile, from when I joined the Navy my mother was always on my case (bless her!). She sounded a little like this, on repeat.

"Save your money, Marcus, save your money."

With fondness, the advice stuck and I did save, just as readily as I helped out with household chores without too much questioning.

I remember my first Christmas leave period in 1998. By the time I'd finished my category training, I'd saved enough to be able to put down a $15,000 deposit on a property. Back then that was a 10% deposit plus costs to buy a property. Back over to my Mum...

"Okay Marcus, let's go look for a property."

I remember feeling excited and freaked out at the same time.

Let me take you through my first property deal.

MY FIRST PROPERTY PURCHASE

I bought a vacant block in an older established location in beautiful Currimundi in Queensland's Sunshine Coast for $58,000. I then constructed a project home - a 4 bed rooms, 2 bath rooms, and double garage house for $68,000. That was back in 1998. Yep. That's how much building costs have gone up!

So my loan was about $120,000 and interest rates were about 5%. With the holding costs I was negatively geared before tax breaks (at a loss) after I received rental income.

The brand new property was attractive to reliable, good paying family tenants. One family loved it so much they paid rent for 7 years! The property rented for $120 per week in 1999, which was slightly negatively geared at $2,500 per annum. That was $58 per week.

Over the 11 years that I had the property I only had four groups of tenants. This doesn't happen all the time but when it does, you're cheering!

Initially I didn't claim depreciation. I didn't know you could. Regardless, the investment was manageable. At the time I was earning $43,000 per annum as a Marine Technician in the Navy.

Here's where the right property, in the right location got me. I sold the property for $430,000 in 2010, a cruisy $300,000 capital gain. Imagine rolling that out a couple of times!

CURRIMUNDI QLD (4 BED 2 BATH 2 GARAGE)

Purchase Year	1998
Purchase Price	$135,000
Land	$58,000
Building	$77,000
Initial Investment	
10% Deposit	$13,500
Costs with purchase	$2,500
Total	$16,000
Out Goings	
Debt or loan amount	
/interest rate	$121,500
@ 6.5%	
Interest Only	$6,240
Expenses	$4,000
Total	$10,240
Income	
1999 Rent	$120 p/w
2010 Rent	$430 p/w

REALISED RETURN

Gross Rental Return 1998	4.95%
Sales Price 1998	$135,000
Gross Rental Return	
on Value - 2010	5.0%
Sales price 2010	$435,000
Capital Gain (Gross)	$300,000
Capital Gain (Net)	
Selling costs	$14,500
Net Capital Gains Tax	$150,000

KNOWLEDGE AND BELIEF GREW A PROPERTY PORTFOLIO

The second collective pivotal points in my life came when I started attending presentations and reading books - downloading information just like you are.

The more I learned, the more encouraged I was to keep going. Inspiring speakers ignited ideas like building wealth to leave a legacy. I was caught – happily.

Before I knew it I had three investment properties under my cap. The more I learnt from expert mentors, the more properties I bought. I grew my portfolio to seven properties in a short space of time. These mentors passed on their legacy in the form of knowledge and belief. That's all it took to keep me going.

Comparatively, I'm a small fish in a big ocean compared to other self made auto biographers. Yet, the deals I have landed have netted me a lifestyle better than I ever imagined. I could never have achieved this if I hadn't started saving my cash early, and grabbed the opportunities in front of me.

I've mentioned this earlier, but I'll share it again in the hope it inspires you to action.

LESSONS FROM MY EXPERIENCES – FOR YOU TO LEARN FROM

Your property investment strategy will be unique to you. It's super personal. Everyone has a unique financial and lifestyle position. I've learned loads, but here is what's front of mind before we get our teeth into the seven step SOP to successfully invest in property:

Lesson #1: you need a steady income and savings to grow wealth

It was a secure income and a commitment to saving some cash that got me my first property. These are non-negotiable check boxes. As soon as you have a secure job and a steady income, a good rule of thumb is to set aside 10% of your wage right from the first salary deposit. That said, it is never too late to start a savings plan.

Lesson #2: your investment strategy is super personal

The bridge you need to get you from your current financial position to your destination will be different from mine, and different from your mates.

> I put in the hard yards early. Now I live a life where I surf when I want to, work when I want to, live where and how I want to, and spend as much time with my young family as I want to.
> – Marcus Westnedge

Don't get fixated on a property. Focus on where you want that property to get you – your personal goals. While you may have a mate that is determined to retire from the workforce by the time he's forty, your personal goal may be a career change over the next few years. You'll both need very different property investment strategies to fund the life you want to live. Look for a property deal that has the right criteria to contribute to getting you to your goal, as part of your personal investment strategy.

Lesson #3: purchase an investment property when you can

As soon as I had my 10% deposit, I took the plunge and invested – thanks to encouragement from my personal mentor (Mum). One of the most common questions investors ask me is *when* they should buy an investment property. One of my earliest mentors passed on this wise response, "...when you can." If you have a deposit, and you've done your research, do the deal. Don't wait. Property investment is all about time over target - time in the market. The best gains are made over the longer term of 10 to 15 years. That's where I am right now.

Lesson #4: capital gain potential must be based on tried and tested criteria

As you've read, my first investment property attracted $300,000 capital growth. I put this down to a combination of factors starting with some good help from my Mum. What also helped was being in the market for the long term along with good support from the property manager. Supply and demand is the foundation of basic economic policy. Location is critical and I base this on tried and tested property investment criteria. We'll explore this in more depth later on in this guide.

Lesson #5: invest or buy a house to live in first?

Another question that pops up regularly is:

'Should I invest first or purchase my Principle Place of Residence (PPR) first?'

A house bought for you to live in will soak up your ability to service other loans or investments. In technical terms this is called your debt to service ratio. We'll explore this more later.

Buying a property investment requires a smaller deposit to secure a bigger loan (better leverage which is also known as your Loan to Value ratio (LVR) – more about this later). An investment property also means you can use rental income to pay for the holding costs to maintain the property. Along with taxation breaks, you'll be in front faster in five years time than if you're still paying down interest on the home you're living in and paying out money to maintain.

I'm speaking from experience. There is a lot of data supporting the belief that over the longer term you'll be in a better financial position if you invest first.

That is my challenge to you. Look into it. You may be surprised by what you discover.

Until you have gone through the process yourself it's really hard to know what to do. You may have read a bunch of books on the subject but still worry about making the wrong decision.

Now, imagine making the right decisions! Go back with me and think about a decision you've made in your life that was a real game changer. It may have been a relationship; career or financial decision. Remember, at 17 and even at 20, I didn't have a clue.

In retrospect, and even knowing what I know now, I believe whole-heartedly that my first investment was the best one. And the principles behind buying it, still apply to the investment decisions I make today, and coach others on.

Don't underestimate the possibilities that are ahead for you!

PART 3

Your 7 Step SOP to Successfully Invest in Property

Being ex-military, I know how valuable your time is. The following is the step by step process that I didn't have when I was in your shoes, and all between the covers of one portable book.

I've been in your shoes. I know you're standing on a mountain of opportunity to reach your goals. You can achieve financial independence from a Defence Force career and pass on your financial savvy to the next generation. All it takes is a little bit of education and a positive shift in thinking.

Make sure you pack this guide in with your gear on your next posting and start planning for your future!

MAKE A COMMITMENT TO YOUR FUTURE RIGHT NOW

As you work through each step you will be asked to commit to completing tasks along the way.

Before we get started, here is what I expect from you. I know you're a high performer – you wouldn't be reading this otherwise – and here is what I expect from someone like you. As you work through this SOP you will demonstrate:

- **Accountability:** you'll do what you say you're going to do
- **Openness and honesty:** you'll be real and authentic to yourself
- **High standards:** you'll push through to give this your personal best
- **Continuous improvement:** you'll measure your progress, and continue to refine and improve.

Set aside some distraction free time so you can set yourself up for a great future. Turn your phone off. Grab a pen and some paper, or your favourite online note app.

Step 1: Set goals that help define your future

Congratulations for getting stuck in to kicking along your property investment career. Let's get started.

You are about to:

- mind map your financial and lifestyle goals
- design your ideal lifestyle
- define what wealth means to you and why it matters
- define your goal setting strategy via a well formed outcome
- start your personal action plan
- find a mentor.

Total reading time 20 – 25 minutes; exercises 1.5 to 2 hours

It might sound a lot, but by breaking this down together – you may surprise yourself.

Mind map your lifestyle and financial goals

> *"If you want to live a happy life, tie it to a goal, not to people or things."*
> *– Albert Einstein*

Imagine your life three, five and ten years from now. What would your ideal lifestyle look like? What does an ideal weekend, or work week look like now? Where are you living? Who are you living with? Who do you mostly spend your time with? What do your finances look like? How are you spending your free time? What state are you in physically and spiritually? What is most important to you? How much free time would you like to have?

Give yourself plenty of time to indulge in this task. It is the foundation of your personal property investment strategy.

Design your ideal lifestyle

By completing the mind mapping exercise above, you've set goals by starting with where you want to get to. At the same time you've started designing your ideal lifestyle.

Once you've got your mind map down, ask yourself the following:

- Do these goals represent a true reflection of my ideal lifestyle?
- Why do I need to build wealth to live this way?
- Will I pursue and achieve this future?
- Will this be a fulfilling or meaningful lifestyle? Will it give me a sense of purpose?

Take your mind mapping a step further. As you imagine your ideal lifestyle, bring in your five senses too. What does it taste like, smell like, sound like? Visualisations that include sensations are powerful motivators.

⚒ : Time to mind map! Write each lifestyle and financial goal down in the middle of one page. Circle it. Then ask yourself why; how; and what – with each answer on a new branch. Keep going until you have an exhaustive list. Keep it to one central goal per page.

⚒ : There are plenty of free mind mapping apps available online. FreeMind is one example – FreeMind.sourceforge.net > Wiki > Index > Download

⚒ : Write yourself a paragraph or two on your future lifestyle. I've seen some fun examples of this where people write a letter to their 30, 40 or 50 year old self!

⚒ : Write down where you are now as well as what is stopping you from living your ideal lifestyle right now.

Define what wealth means to you and why it matters

Wealth is subjective. It is the means you need to enjoy a lifestyle aligned with your values and desires. Your values and desires are unique to you. You need to find your own definition of wealth.

The mind mapping exercise along with the paragraph you've written on your future lifestyle should help you define your own definition of wealth. Once you understand 'the why' and feel a desire to reach your goals, you are well on your way to achieving them.

🐦 **Question:** #DearMarcus WHERE DO I START?!!

🐦 **Reply:** Start with the end in mind. This sets your strategy. Where do you want to be in the future? Where are you now? What do you need to do to get there?

> "Whatever wealth means to you, it will have a completely different meaning for someone else."
> – Your mentor, Marcus.

Many of the great visionaries throughout time started with a clear image of the future. I believe this is the key to setting a plan in place that will succeed. Now it's your turn to uncover your motivational factors and desire for building wealth.

You'll find 'your why' can change as you move through different life cycles, over time. Personally, I've found that keeping your wealth building strategy simple works best. That's why residential property investment has worked for me, and many others.

If you're always clear on where you're heading and why, you will succeed in building wealth to fund your goals. Over time, growing wealth happens as a matter of course with the right property criteria backing your decisions. It isn't the fastest method out there, but it works – it's slow but sure; or perhaps sure but slow.

Define your goal setting strategy: the well formed outcome

The goal setting strategy I am about to introduce to you – the *Well Formed Outcome* – is one of the most powerful techniques out there for propelling people to success.

A well formed outcome is a goal that fits in with all the aspects of your life – not just financial. Defining the plan to reach your goals takes all the facets of your lifestyle into consideration. Without doing this, a goal is a vague dream that could apply to anyone. This process is about making your outcomes, personal.

A well formed outcome will set your direction, or your plan of attack – your personal campaign strategy to hit each of your targets. It is a thoughtful goal setting strategy. With action, well formed outcomes are a potent motivator.

> "Realize what you really want. It stops you from chasing butterflies and puts you to work digging gold."
> - William Moulton Marsden, 19th century Psychologist and author.

Through the tasks preceding this page, you've already defined a range of future goals that consider all the aspects of your life, what wealth means to you and where you are right now.

🔧 : Take a couple of minutes to write down
1) what wealth means to you; and 2) why you want to build wealth.

Now you have this you need a plan of how to reach those goals from where you are right now. Now it's your turn!

Work through it as often as you need. I sometimes use this process a few times in a week with stuff I'm working on. I've found it a great tool to motivate and set very powerful goals.

By having a goal-setting plan you bridge the gap between today's dreams and tomorrow's reality and make it personal. The practice of committing goals to paper has been found to be associated with higher lifetime earnings than someone that doesn't. Motivated?

Start your personal action plan

The Personal Action Plan you're about to complete is a powerful tool for tracking progress toward your goals.

Use the Personal Action Plan as a living document that you'll visit, review and update regularly. Print it out and make it a visual reminder too. This will take the work you've already completed and condense it into a plan you can monitor.

> "You will become as small as your controlling desire; as great as your dominant aspiration." – James Allen, 19th century British author

Find a mentor

I don't believe I would have achieved what I have today without the support of a mentor to encourage me to get started, and a range of mentors that have guided and inspired me along the way.

A mentor is ideally someone you hold in high regard that shares similar ideals and values. The most effective mentor is someone that has walked the path of achieving their goals. Knowledge acquired through real life experience and lessons learned aren't found by 'Googling'.

Mentors can sometimes find you. It's a synergistic relationship with mutual benefits. Mentors can expedite the whole process and help you explore ways to fill the gaps from now to where you want to be. You'll discover different thinking patterns and may change the way you think about building wealth through osmosis.

⚒ : Complete the goal setting worksheet for each of your goals.

⚒ : Go to this link to access your goal setting worksheet – capitalproperties.com.au > Resources and Tools > Psychology of Success

....

⚒ : Complete your personal action plan.

....

⚒ : Go to the investor tools section of capitalproperties.com.au > Resources and Tools > Investor Tools & Apps and download 'Brainstorm your lifestyle goals' (Personal Action Sheet) and 'Track your lifestyle and financial goals' (Personal Action Plan).

....

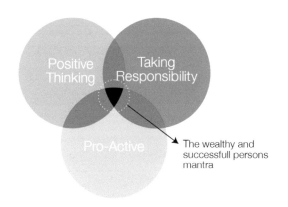

The wealthy and successfull persons mantra

Research has found that wealthy people often share similar thinking traits including:

- thinking positively

- taking responsibility for where they are now and where they want to go

- being proactive.

My mentors have been people that don't wait unnecessarily, they're effective and they do more than just get the job done.

Congratulations! You've stayed the course and have completed Step 1. Keep going.

Step 2: Access your resources

Congratulations for getting stuck in to kicking along your property investment career. Let's get started.

You are about to:

- find out exactly where you are financially

- work out the deposit you need to borrow for an investment property

- prepare an Assets and Liabilities worksheet

- get a copy of your credit file

- contact a finance broker to find out what your borrowing capacity is

Total reading time 20 – 25 minutes; exercises 1.5 to 2 hours

Find out exactly where you are financially

Now you know where you want to go to, you now need to understand where you are today – the other side of the bridge that you're building. Here's how.

> *#StandEasyTip 1: start tracking money in and money out.*

Today is the day that you limit the amount of money you withdraw from your cash account each week. Set up a simple budget spreadsheet to show money coming in, and how much is going out every week. You'll be surprised at how simply tracking your finances can motivate you to slow up on spending.

Maintaining a budget worksheet will help you analyse where you are now, and project what your financial situation looks like in the future.

> "Every great journey starts with a single step, start yours today with a budget."
> – Marcus Westnedge

⚒ : Think about your networks including work mates, colleagues, family and community. Shortlist some potential mentors you could reach out to.

#StandEasyTip 2: use credit cards and pay the full balance every month

Stop withdrawing cash, and start paying as much as you can by credit card. Importantly you must then pay the full balance owing on the credit card every month. By using credit for all your regular expenses, you'll quickly get a view of your average expenditure every month.

#StandEasyTip 3: keep ship shape records and make it a habit

From the moment you start thinking about buying property for investment, you need to start filing everything. Keep all of your receipts and documentation in one well organised spot. The old school expanding files from office stationery suppliers is a great start – or a sturdy binder with loads of plastic sleeves and tabs. Come tax time, you and your accountant will be thankful for this advice.

#StandEasyTip 4: start saving right now and make it a habit

This is a non negotiable action you must take if you want to set yourself up to be financially independent. Here is how you can start saving for the deposit on a property:

- Set a target savings goal of a minimum of $25,000. That is your starting point to cover a 5% deposit plus all the associated fees for a lower entry level property of $350,000. While the figures below are a guide only, here's how that could look:

Deposit %	5%*	10%*	20%
Purchase price:	$350,000	$350,000	$350,000
Deposit:	$17,500	$35,000	$70,000
Stamp duty^:	$2,600	$2,600	$2,600
Solicitor's fees:	$1,500	$1,500	$1,500
Bank fees:	$1,500	$1,500	$1,500
Miscellaneous fees:	$1,000	$1,000	$1,000
Total deposit and costs:	$24,100	$41,600	$76,600

* Lenders mortgage insurance will be payable > www.genworth.com.au

^ This stamp duty is based from the land only (As part of a house and land package) and is an estimate this varies from state to state.

- Start putting aside at least $150 every week in to cash savings. Ideally $320 every week will see you reach your savings target in just over a year and a half. Believe me a year and a half goes very quickly when you have a goal to reach!

: Kick off your new budget planner right now.

: Download and save Capital Properties' Budget Spending Worksheet. Go to the Investor Tools section of capitalproperties.com.au > Resources & Tools > Investor Tools & Apps.

- Ask family and friends to give cash for gifts rather than stuff you don't really need – put those cash gifts straight into your savings account to give it a boost.

  #StandEasyTip 5: think outside of the square

If you have a stable income and at least $5,000 in savings, and parents with equity in their principal place of residence, with their support you may qualify for a guarantor loan. As you build equity in the property you can remove your parents as guarantors, and gain their respect! Imagine having this head start in your property investment career.

Work out the deposit you need to borrow for the right investment property

It's time to get a little technical. Your loan to value ratio (LVR) is the amount you are borrowing as a percentage of the value of the property you're using as security for the loan. For example a 90% LVR means you are handing over a 10% deposit to your lender the 90% is the loan hence the loan to the value. A 10% deposit plus enough money to cover all your fees is all you need to get started in most cases. The additional fees equates to roughly 5% of the value of the property – a combined total of 10% of the purchase price of the property plus costs.

If you don't have a spare $45K sitting around, you've still got this! Here's what you need to do next.

Ask yourself:

- How much money do you need to save every week over the next twelve to twenty four months to reach your target deposit?

- What other funding or financial resources might be available to you? This could include assets you can sell; family, friends or mentors that can give you a hand up or equity they have that they could offer to go guarantor on a loan to get you started.

Prepare an Assets and Liabilities spreadsheet

Banks and other lenders use some form of an asset and liabilities spreadsheet as part of assessing how much money they are prepared to risk lending to you.

Having an Assets and Liabilities spreadsheet prepared ahead of time is a great way to stay on top of your personal debts and repayments, interest rates and loan terms for personal debts or bad debts.

It's time to get technical again. Before a bank or lender hands over money to you to invest they want to understand what your debt to service ratio is.

> "Income producing assets – like the right investment property - put money in your pocket. Depreciating assets can be a liability taking money straight out of your back pocket."

⚒ : If you're not storing all your financial bits and pieces in one filing spot, head out to a stationery supply store and buy a brand new filing system – expanding file or binder with inserts – and start filing

⚒ : Write down your answers to the questions above.

If you have a job you enjoy, and the means to fund an investment loan, all you need is some help to get your foot in the door. Remember, as the value of your property and the equity grows, you're saving as well as reducing your tax bill.

In simple terms, they need to know that you will have enough cash flow left over, after you pay all your regular debt commitments, to meet their repayments. I saw many of my Defence mates lured into the world of new cars and expensive toys before they have the savings. Coming back cashed up from operational deployments was a common trigger for 'bad debt' purchases. 'Bad debt' is when you borrow money to buy an asset that reduces in value over time - depreciates. For bankers and lenders, bad debt that affects your ability to repay an investment loan, will wipe the warm smiles from their faces!

Some 'bad assets' reduce in value faster than the rate you can pay down the debt owing on them. Be careful. Think ahead to your future goals every time you consider buying something new.

Get a copy of your credit file

If you've ever had a credit card, mobile phone or applied for finance, you will have a credit history or 'credit file' that will influence your ability to borrow money for an investment property.

Even if you don't think you have a credit history, I would recommend that you request a copy anyway to make sure your file is clear. It doesn't cost anything to get a copy.

Leaving a bill unpaid for longer than three months is a common reason for having a credit history default applied that isn't looked upon favourably by lenders. The blip can stay on our file for up to five years. So here's a tip, prioritise staying up to date with your bill payments, always.

If you do have a questionable credit file, all is not lost. By knowing this before you approach a lender to borrow for an investment property, you can investigate and depending on the circumstances you may be able to request to have the default cleared from your credit history.

Contact a finance broker to find out what your borrowing capacity is

Finance brokers love a switched-on borrower. Having your records ship shape and awareness of your credit history will definitely give a great first impression.

By establishing your borrowing power with a finance broker before you approach a seller – and having evidence of 'pre-approval' or 'conditional approval', your offer will be far more appealing than other offers from the sellers view.

⚒ : Get a clear view on how a bank or lender would view your current assets and liabilities. Put aside some time to complete the Assets and Liabilities worksheet.

⚒ : Download and save Capital Properties' Assets and Liabilities worksheet. Go to the investor tools section of capitalproperties.com.au > Resources & Tools > Investor Tools & Apps.

⚒ : To get a copy of your credit file, visit mycreditfile.com.au > products and services > mycreditfile.com.au

⚒ : If you've completed all the action steps leading up to this point, it is time to book in to see your finance broker and find out how much money you can borrow.

The calculations your broker will work through are:

- Loan to value ratio (LVR)
- Debt to service ration (DSR)
- Lenders Mortgage Insurance (LMI)
- Interest only versus Principle and Interest

You'll find definitions of these calculations in the Appendix of this book.

Once you find a good finance broker, add them to your advisory team as you grow your property portfolio.

Step 3: Develop your strategy

Congratulations for getting this far. You should now have a very clear understanding of where you are right now financially. Keep going.

Based on the work you've completed so far you are about to:

- ◆ *start developing your property investment strategy*
- ◆ *work out how much you want to be worth when you retire*
- ◆ *define how much risk you are willing to live with*
- ◆ *build a team of experts around you.*

As part of Step 2, we've got you off to your finance broker already, before delving into the detail of your property investment strategy.

We've done that intentionally because one of the key principles of success in property investment is getting started early. The earlier you invest, the greater the rewards. Once you're on your way to purchasing your first investment property, it is time to plan the rest of your life!

Start developing your property investment strategy

Your property investment strategy will be loosely built around your answers to the following questions, your:

- **Risk tolerance: low, medium or high. How much risk are you willing to take on?**
  - How long have you been employed?
  - How long do you plan to work with the Australian Defence Forces?
- **Return needs: do you need to focus on income or growth?**
  - How old are you?
  - What age would you like to retire from salaried employment commitments?
  - What do you want to be worth in terms of net assets, when you retire?
- **Investment time frame:**
  - Is there a point when you might need additional cash flow? For example, planning a family or a career change and relying on only one income for a time.

   - What sort of income do you want to support the retirement lifestyle you want to live?
- **Tax position: what tax bracket are you in?**
   - If you're paying tax at the high end, it may be an idea to invest in assets where the return is free from tax. The equity growth property can give will be tax free until you crystallise the asset and sell them.
- **Dependants:** do other people rely on you for financial support?
   - This will impact the type of investments that will work best for you. For example, someone with five children will have a different strategy to someone who is single with no dependants.

If you're early in your career, that is great! It is never too early to get started. From a finance lender's view, once you have successfully made it through your employment probation period you become a more favourable candidate for being able to finance loan repayments.

If you have already bought property, keep going! Continue maintaining a good savings pattern and you can keep building your wealth.

What do you want your net assets to be worth when you retire?

Goal setting puts you on the 110 km per hour freeway versus the 80 km per hour main road. The freeway will see you reach your destination faster, with fewer disruptions and less wear and tear!

To avoid plodding along without any destination in sight, you need to know what you're aiming for. What I mean by this is what net value of assets would you like to be worth when you retire? For example, if you sold everything how much would you have left over once all expenses were paid, including debts and taxes? Start from this figure, and plan your strategy around it.

#Special note: Make sure that you consider inflation. The value of money can roughly halve in buying power every decade. For example, $100 worth of groceries ten years ago may have filled your shopping trolley but it won't go that far today.

So if you're 25 today, and would like to retire by the time you're 50 years old and aiming for a total net asset value of $1.5 million of property (returning you rental income), you need to plan your strategy on a goal of achieving a $8 million property portfolio in 25 years time.

Stay with me! This may sound like a lot right now, but along the way you'll be building equity, your properties will be growing in capital value and you'll be receiving rental income and tax breaks.

How much risk are you prepared to live with?

As you build out your strategy you need to consider how much risk you are comfortable with living with. Here are some of the questions you need to consider:

- How much of a deposit are you able to, or prepared to, put down on your property purchases?
- What is the minimum and maximum purchase price you are prepared to commit to?
- How much buffer do you want to have available to cover property related expenses and rental vacancies and other ad hoc expenses?

: Grab some scrap paper for now and do some number crunching. Start by answering the questions on the previous page.

#StandEasyTip: To help you work out the amount you're prepared to borrow for an investment property, refocus on your goals.

Then, zoom out and take an aerial view of the whole of Australia. Consider which capital city market shows good potential based on the 'Australian Market Overview' indicators which we'll cover shortly in step 4. Then zoom in on a local area to consider 'Property Location Criteria' which we'll also consider as part of step 4. Once you've identified a local area, you can then run servicing calculations 'Cash Flow Analysis' on specific properties for affordability which we'll go into more detail in step 5.

That will then give you an idea of the purchase price of a good investment property. Then you can start crunching numbers.

The most effective way to manage risk in property investing is to be a switched-on investor with an appetite for educating yourself on property investment.

Here are some ideas to manage property investment risk.

To eliminate unexpected expense related risks relevant to newly constructed or to-be constructed property:

- enter into a fixed price, lump sum contract
- agree on a guaranteed build time in the contract
- ask for warranties on appliances
- make sure the contract is subject to finance approval.
- choose a fixed interest rate loan.

To control the risk of choosing the right investment property:

- choose a good design and specification
- check your builder's track record before signing a contract
- target a specific rental market
- make sure the location criteria is good for property investment
- choose a stand-alone finance structure, if possible.

To transfer or share the risk:

- bring on an expert team including mentors
- have the lender provide an independent valuation
- take out insurances:
    - title
    - building
    - landlord.
- Invest for the longer term

Once a decision is made you need to monitor and manage risk by:

- making a research based decision and monitoring it
- knowing the development holding costs
- monitoring interest rates, they'll move up and down
- keeping up-to-date with lending policy changes.

Build a team of experts around you.

You can't do this on your own. I can't do this on my own and I've had decades of experience!

Here is a list of the expertise you need to surround yourself with:

- **A real estate agent:** to transact the property purchase.

- **A conveyancer:** a specialist solicitor with expertise in conveyancing to help you cover off legalities.

- **A mortgage broker:** a broker with investment property expertise to help you finance the property and find the most effective loan to meet your goals.

- **A real estate agent with property management expertise:** in your Defence lifestyle you need to have a professional manage your property to find good tenants and manage the risks associated with tenancy / landlord agreements.

- **A tax accountant:** an accountant that specialises in investment property and all that is claimable will help maximise your cash flow, by minimising your tax bill.

- **A quantity surveyor:** to help you estimate construction costs for depreciation purposes.

- **Land developers:** a good network of land developers Australia wide can get you in the know as to what good property investments are about to hit the market.

- **Builders:** you need to find builders with a balanced approach to quality, cost, design and specifications. The overall quality needs to be fit for purpose and attractive, but not over the top.

- **Property insurances:** the right insurance will help you manage property investment risks. It is mandatory to have building insurance, and landlord insurance is highly recommended.

- **Financial planner:** a good written financial plan will help you get a clear understanding of your financial goals, how you'll reach them, and how you're tracking. A financial planner will have a holistic view of your finances, from personal insurances through to diversified investments.

This is your wealth building team. Make sure that even as your knowledge grows, that the team you have around you is always smarter than you if you want to keep growing your wealth.

A special note on real estate agents

You really need to find an agent interested in finding you a property based on your goals and your current financial position. That's unusual for an agent. Yet investors need an agent that has their interests . That's why we exist. We offer an opportunity for you to learn about property investment before you start. We offer mentoring and will help you build your knowledge of property investment. Having a mentor is a great way to move out of the slow lane and learn how to take the most efficient routes to get to your destination.

Having a great team around you makes for a much smoother, more pleasant, less nerve wracking experience – you'll enjoy it more. Albert Einstein wrote a well documented letter to his son that basically said that the best way to learn is do something that you really enjoy.

✗ : Contact us at Capital Properties and come and meet the team. Keep reading, but we can help bring this guide to life for you. Capitalproperties.com.au > Contact.

Step 4: Research | location and asset class

Now that you understand the financial goals you want your strategy to drive, it is time to research the location and type of property to fit your strategy. Choosing the right location and then the right property is critical to the success of your strategy.

Based on the work you've completed so far you are about to learn more about:

- *timing the property market*
- *investment property selection criteria*
- *the builder and the importance of the right design to target the right tenants*
- *turnkey packages as a great solution for Defence investors.*

Timing the property market

Timing the Australian property market or cycles is a key factor in kicking off your property research. You need to know when and where to enter a property market for growth. Getting it right comes down to education, knowledge and research.

#StandEasyTip 1: Effective research from good solid reliable sources is the only way to get the timing right.

You'll need to do some comparative research based on twelve months before. Start with researching current capital growth in each state based on median house prices. Look at demand in terms of sales activity. Is demand high or low? You also need to consider the supply of land; rental demand; the trend in building approvals; and the days on the market until property is sold. Find out the overall health of the state in terms of employment, planning, and infrastructure; compared with the other states.

Being a switched-on investor is all about seizing an opportunity before it becomes commercially advertised. If you've seen a house and land package in the locality you're looking in, in a property investor magazine or newspaper, the opportunity is already gone.

Your goal is to become someone 'in the know' – switched-on. You can achieve this by being educated about the different markets within Australia and what drives them. Understanding the key indicators will drive you to make a decision to give you the highest return.

Economists use loads of different indicators to provide property market updates. I'll try and simplify it for you. Is that a sigh of relief I hear?!

Investment property selection criteria

Once you've got your hands on some good quality data about the Australian capital city property market, here are the key factors you need to consider in choosing a capital city market that suits your goals.

Based on current median house prices, which capital cities are affordable?

Understanding how much you can afford, will help you narrow down your property market.

By looking at the median house price of each capital city, you'll be able to determine which of these markets is in your reach. This will give you a solid idea of where to start, and on what price represents a good entry point.

What does the historical capital growth data tell you?

Potential for capital growth – that means you will be able to unlock equity down the track to grow your portfolio – is a key factor to consider.

Track the median house prices of the specific market you are looking to enter. Look at property market data that shows growth right now. Target a steady, average annual capital growth of between 3% and 9%. While higher capital growth seems attractive, you don't want to invest in an area that has already reached its peak and is now overvalued – it's too risky.

Is population growth shifting and why?

Population is a key indicator of demand for a particular property market. Population growth will be impacted by overseas and interstate migration, and natural birth and attrition rates – births and deaths.

Population shifts in a property market are a strong indicator of longer term, sustained demand, and in turn capital growth driven by demand.

The big question is what makes it attractive for people to live in a particular suburb in a major capital city or regional centre?

Affordability is a driving factor of demand in the current property market. Right now, most major capital cities are pushing beyond the half a million median price threshold.

Well-planned government and private infrastructure projects can also attract new residents and grow families, particularly if a location is in high demand and infrastructure is keeping up with, or staying ahead of, population growth.

In an already built up and mature area, populations can max out and in some cases, decline. If urban development or infill has already taken place, and there is no room for the population to grow, population growth will stall. Make sure to take this in to consideration.

What you're looking for here is evidence of sure but steady population growth over the medium term, and enough land and planned infrastructure to support population growth.

Are government and private projects prioritising infrastructure spending?

Infrastructure is the physical structures or facilities needed to support a local population such as shopping centres; convenience stores; freeways, roads, roundabouts and other traffic control systems; private and public transport; hospitals and medical centres; schools, child care and ageing care facilities; and recreational grounds and facilities.

Infrastructure funded by government and private investing is largely driven by population shifts.

An emerging area with funded projects due to be delivered in the medium term of 5 to 10 years; or an area where demographics are shifting, referred as gentrification or urban renewal, both indicate positive property market criteria worthy of exploring further.

Check out the state government and local government websites to research infrastructure projects in the pipeline. The prioritisation of short, medium and longer term investment projects will generally align with population growth of the area.

What you're looking for is evidence of enough existing infrastructure for now as well as planned infrastructure projects in the short and medium term. This means there is confidence that the area will be a growth corridor.

How are the states property sales looking as an indicator of supply and demand?

Housing supply is driven by land availability, construction costs and profitability for developers.

Infrastructure costs such as water, power, sewerage and public transport can impact housing supply.

Housing demand is driven by the number and type of households looking for housing. Demand is driven by factors such as household income, employment trends, preferences for house size, location, preferred type of property and current interest rates.

The supply and demand of the property sales market of a specific area can be subjective. The Australian Bureau of Statistics (ABS) population figures can lag the number of properties listed on real estate websites. However, putting the two figures side by side can give you a general feel of the current sales market as a ration of the population.

The lag between the ABS population statistics and dwelling starts could be due to the time it takes for building supply to start hitting the market. Planning, design, approvals and construction time frames all need to happen in the lead up to a property being listed. You are best to enlist the guidance of an expert in exploring these criteria.

By understanding the demand, you can attract good quality stable tenants for long tenures by designing a new build to suit the demographics driving the demand.

How is the rental market looking on return and vacancies?

The best way to gauge rents for specific property markets is to talk to local agents working in the area you're looking to invest in.

As a switched-on investor, what you're looking for is a low vacancy rate and high rental demand. Around 3% is a normal vacancy rate. Vacancy rates will vary over time so you will need to monitor regularly.

> #StandEasyTip 2: Get three or more rental appraisals done.

When talking to the agent ask how many properties they manage as opposed the amount of properties they currently have advertised for lease.

The number of rental properties being managed will give you a good sense of vacancy rates. There are free tools available to explore this criteria further, such as SQM Research vacancy rate (SQM Research > Free Property Data > Research Reports > Vacancy Rates.

This is just a starting point. We just wanted to share some of the basics to help you on your way. Make informed property investment decisions. Expert guidance will move you closer to your goals with more certainty and speed.

Is the rental yield showing a good return?

If you've applied all the other criteria we've talked about so far, a rental return of at least 4% to 6% will give you enough income to support the investment property purchase.

How can you choose a property to minimise your tax bill?

The government incentivises new construction by offering tax deductions to cover off set the wear and tear on an income producing property asset – depreciation.

You can claim depreciation of a newly constructed investment property against your taxable income at a higher rate than a property that is older.

Invest in a new build to maximise your cash flow and reduce your tax bill.

How else can you gain a lender's confidence in loaning you money?

A valuation closer to the purchase price on the property you are asking to borrow money for will give you a better chance of getting the deal financed and settled. A valuation that comes in at the higher end of what the property is worth lowers the risk for the lender – and for you!

A good valuation of the property you want to purchase is the foundation of your property investment strategy.

Take a satellite view, not a street view

Every decision you make from here on is for the longer term and calls on you to take a view from above, not down on street level. You can't look at any of the criteria above in isolation. You need to checklist that you have covered off all of these criteria not just one or a few. Why? Because you will need income producing assets to fund the lifestyle you're aspiring to enjoy earlier, rather than later.

The builder: the importance of the right design to target the right tenants

From my experience having a good team in place, including a good builder is gold. A builder with a good track record gives me a lot of confidence in a property being constructed for investment.

What are you looking for in a builder?

You'll get a sense of a builder's track record by finding out how many projects they've built in the past, and how many starts they can do at any one time. This indicates how cashed up the builder is, minimising the risk of the builder going bust halfway through your project.

Top tier land developers have strict building guidelines and a proven track record so ideally you want your builder to be one that has worked tightly with proven land developers. If you've already settled on your land and the builder is working with a land developer for the first time there could be delays in getting the design right for the estate. Ouch. Any delay can eat into your cash flow.

You also want to find a builder that understands that while the specifications don't need to be on the high end, the finish needs to attract reliable, good paying tenants.

✖ : Take a look at some of the property market research data available. Request the latest copy of the Australian Property Market Report; and refer to the property clock section.
Go to capitalproperties.com.au > Resources & Tools >

Australian Property Market Report

Go to capitalproperties.com.au > Resources & Tools > Investor tools & apps >

Australian Market Overview

Property Selection Criteria

What do the right tenants look like?

The secret to success of any business venture is that you are offering a product or service attractive to your target market. The house you build should intentionally be designed to attract your ideal tenant.

> *#StandEasyTip 3: Who is your ideal tenant? Is it a house full of itinerant students? Or is it restless young single people? Think about cash flow, stability, reliability and security.*

Your ideal tenant is a young couple or family in their early to mid 30s that have a child or two and want to establish themselves in your home for the medium term to see their children through their school years.

A young couple or family tends to be statistically more stable and longer term focused in their leasing arrangements. They also tend to be reliable for timely rental payments.

By targeting this demographic, you will secure longer term tenants. Less tenant turnover means less of your cash being paid out to your property manager for advertising and re-leasing fees. This gives you a record of consistent rental income to service your loans which in turn will help you leverage and build your property portfolio.

By looking after your tenants through good property management and attending to maintenance requests swiftly, you'll be rewarded with tenants that feel a sense of ownership and will go out of their way to look after your property.

What does the right building design look like?

Here is what attracts young couples and families. Houses designed well in the eyes of this demographic have a good flow. The design separates bedrooms from one or two (or more) living areas which may include a media room or study. Affordable two to three bedroom and two bathroom houses are popular with young couples and families with the spare bedroom used for storage or a home office.

For more expensive areas, three bedroom cottages or villa style properties will be sought after for affordable rent. The number of living areas you build into the design will depend on the location and cost of construction.

Turnkey finish properties are the ideal investment solution for Defence personnel

Why?

If your Defence lifestyle is one of being frequently posted away from home, you need a solution that doesn't require you to be hands on.

A turnkey finish means that the property is rent ready and there is nothing left to do. Tenants can move straight into the property after hand over. This is the term you are looking for when you are searching for a property investment opportunity.

Don't be fooled by marketing hooks. In your research, you may find some house and land packages online that seem cheap. That is because the seller wants you to call them to find out more, so that they have an opportunity to talk to you and close the deal. Getting the property to a state where tenants can move in may cost you thousands more on top of the advertised price, and time!

For example:

To get a property to a turnkey finish the cross over (the part of the driveway between the road and the overside of the nature strip); the mail box; the clothes line; and floor coverings all need to be completed and ready for occupancy.

Step 5: Cash flow analysis

The previous section was focused on learning more about the criteria to consider when choosing an investment property. This is section is a working one, so make sure to have your pen and paper, mobile phone or note taking app ready to do some work.

Based on the work you've completed so far you are about to learn more about:

- *how to work out your cash flow position – aka your income and expenses*
- *how to gauge your potential rental income through a rental appraisal*
- *the current interest rate and its impact on your cash flow*
- *calculating the loan amount*
- *factoring in the tax benefits*
- *factoring in holding costs*

At the end of this step, I've provided a simple cash flow example to show you how it all comes together.

How to work out your cash flow position – aka your income

Now that you've potentially chosen or short listed an investment property, it is time to crunch some numbers.

You'll need to determine the projected rental return. To do this, find at least three real estate agents that specialise in property management and request an independent rental appraisal from each agent. This should give you a good indication of the rental return.

Average the three and use that figure as a guide.

> *#StandEasyTip 1: To work out your cash flow position there are a number of variables to consider. You'll need to calculate both your pre-tax and post-tax position.*

The reason for this is that with the right quantity surveyor report the tax benefits can be significant and worth weighing up.

Calculate all the variables on an annual basis, and break down to fortnightly or weekly for the micro view.

Here are the variables you'll need to consider for the property you are considering investing in:

- Your personal income plus the projected rental income
- The purchase price of the property

: Grab some scrap paper or a note taking app and do some number crunching as you work your way through this step. You'll need to be prepared to make some phone calls and start building your property investment team!
"I want to understand how property investment will give me some cash flow."
Go to capitalproperties.com.au > Investor Tools & Apps > Property gearing calculator

---

- The additional purchase costs including stamp duty, solicitors fees, insurances and bank fees
- The amount of deposit you are putting down
- The interest rate range (upper and lower); and the loan terms (how many years)
- Ongoing property expenses including water rates, council rates, insurances, maintenance and rental management fees.

Being able to calculate and understand your cash flow is a key skill and quality for someone who wants to be successful in property investment.

It means being able to understand one third of the overall potential. Research and leverage potential are the other two slices of the successful investment pie.

How to gauge projected rental income through a rental appraisal

Make sure you base your projected rental income on an accurate source.

> *#StandEasyTip 2: To get an idea of your projected rental income jump on to realestate.com.au or domain.com.au and search for a similar property in the same location.*

Comparing similar rental properties online around the same location will give you a good idea of:

- Rental demand: how many similar properties are available for rent?
- Rental income potential: what are landlords asking for rent for similar properties in the location?
- Rental types: what types of properties are available for rent – for example units, townhouses, houses?
- Property agents: this online research may give you an idea of which agents to contact for an independent rental appraisal and potentially, future management of your property / properties.

Then, it's time to contact your shortlist of property management agents and ask for a written rental appraisal.

How to choose a knowledgeable property management agent that can support your strategy, find:

- **a local agent:** this could involve a larger agency with the main office in the city.
- **a licensed and experienced agent**: five plus years in property management experience is good. A multi-tasking profession, in my experience women tend to be great property managers (no offence guys!).
- **an agent with a manageable property portfolio:** to get good service, you don't want to be dealing with an agent that manages hundreds of properties by themselves.
- **a bigger agency:** agencies with 1,000 plus properties under management seem to be better in providing support like research reports on vacancy rates, rental appraisals, and property news articles. Just make sure that the individual agents aren't managing hundreds of properties, to my point above.
- **a discounted management fee:** if you've got multiple properties in one city, you could have one agency looking after all your properties and possibly negotiate on management fees.
- **an informed and responsive office reception:** the way your call is received will give you an insight into the agency and how they operate – from your view, and your tenants'.
- **an agency with a lower vacancy rate:** have the agent prepare a rental appraisal and get some feedback on the market. Ask how many properties he or she manages and how many are currently vacant.

- **a responsive agent:** how readily available is the agent when you try to contact them? If you leave a message asking for a response, how long does it take to get back to you?

Remember that the agent should be acting in your interest. Always remember that.

The current interest rate and its impact on your cash flow

Your cash flow calculation needs to take into account the current interest rate that you'll be paying on your property loan. In calculating the current variable interest rate, take the higher interest rate in calculating your cash flows.

According to the Reserve Bank of Australia (RBA) the banks' variable interest rates hover around 2 to 2.5% above the official cash rate.

Calculating the loan amount

The total amount you will need to borrow needs to cover:

- the purchase price of the property less the deposit
- the purchase costs – such as insurances, solicitors fees and stamp duty

An example is provided at the end of this step.

Factoring in tax benefits

As I mentioned in Step 4, I highly recommend a new construction – in the right location and meeting proven property and location selection criteria mentioned in Step 3 – to maximise the tax benefits available. Tax benefits or tax minimisation, is cash flow.

✕ : Take a moment to get online and have a look at the major banks websites – Westpac, National Australia Bank, Commonwealth Bank and ANZ – to find out what the current variable interest rates are.

✕ : To start building your property investment team, you'll need to do some research to find a taxation accountant that has expertise in residential property investment. Write a short list based on recommendations from investment mentors. We're here to help if you're not sure of how to go about pulling together a good team that you can trust.

✕ : It's time for you to do some research and pull together some calculations. You'll need to set aside some time for some online research or phone calls to local council, insurance providers, 'builders' and local property managers.

Factoring in holding costs

Holding costs are the ongoing costs of owning and maintaining a property as a landlord. You'll need to calculate the total holding costs annually as part of your overall cash flow calculation.

You'll need to do some research on the following costs based on the property you have in mind:

- water rates

- council rates

- insurances – both landlord and building (non strata title)

- maintenance – because your property is new or near new, these should be minimal in the short term (note: Archicentre.com.au is a good source of current property maintenance costs)

- property management fees – dependent on the rental and agent fees

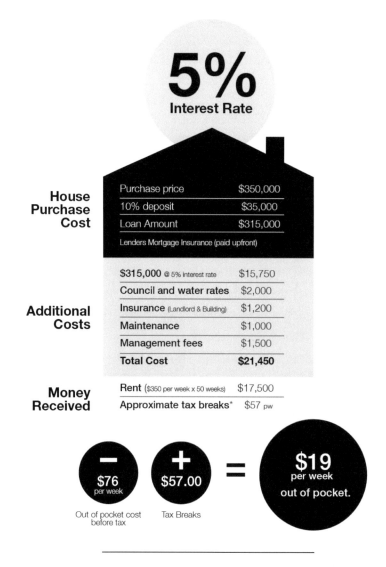

5%
Interest Rate

House Purchase Cost

Purchase price	$350,000
10% deposit	$35,000
Loan Amount	$315,000
Lenders Mortgage Insurance (paid upfront)	

Additional Costs

$315,000 @ 5% interest rate	$15,750
Council and water rates	$2,000
Insurance (Landlord & Building)	$1,200
Maintenance	$1,000
Management fees	$1,500
Total Cost	**$21,450**

Money Received

Rent ($350 per week x 50 weeks)	$17,500
Approximate tax breaks*	$57 pw

− $76 per week
Out of pocket cost before tax

+ $57.00
Tax Breaks

= $19 per week out of pocket.

---

* Approximate tax breaks for an individual:

- Earning $80,000 per annum
- One investment property valued at $350,000 (land $130,000 + build $220,000)
- Achieving a 5% rental return (total rent per annum / purchase price)
- 10% deposit paid
- Based on 5% interest rate

7%
Interest Rate

House Purchase Cost

Purchase price	$350,000
10% deposit	$35,000
Loan Amount	$315,000
Lenders Mortgage Insurance (paid upfront)	

Additional Costs

$337,050 @ 7% interest rate	$22,050
Council and water rates	$2,000
Insurance (Landlord & Building)	$1,200
Maintenance	$1,000
Management fees	$1,500
Total Cost	**$27,750**

Money Received

Rent ($350 per week x 50 weeks)	$17,500
Approximate tax breaks*	$100 pw

$197.00
Out of pocket cost before tax

$100.00
Tax Breaks

$97
per week
out of pocket.

---

* Approximate tax breaks for an individual:

- Earning $80,000 per annum
- One investment property valued at $350,000 (land $130,000 + build $220,000)
- Achieving a 5% rental return (total rent per annum / purchase price)
- 10% deposit paid
- Based on 7% interest rate

Step 6: Settlement | post settlement

Now that you are clear on your cash flow position, and hopefully still smiling, it's time to buy property and have some great tenants move in!

Based on the work you've completed so far you are about to learn more about:

- ◆ *Contracts*
- ◆ *Construction phase*
- ◆ *Handover*
- ◆ *Finding and managing good tenants*
- ◆ *Review*
- ◆ *Keep saving ready to invest in your next property*

Know your contracts and have a licensed conveyancer go over them

Congratulations if you've reached this stage of the exciting journey ahead. Straight up, I am not a licensed conveyancer or solicitor. However based on experience I'll share with you what I know but always, always bring in a licensed conveyancer or solicitor to review the contract when you sign anything.

What is an Expression of Interest (EOI)?

If you've completed all your homework and have found the property that is going to help you reach your goals, you can use an EOI to secure it with minimal risk. An EOI may call on you to pay a small, refundable deposit ($1K to $5K) and it is non-binding. That means if you change your mind, you can verbally cancel the EOI.

How do I cut through the legal speak and jargon of a contract?

Once you enter into an EOI, you'll have around ten to fourteen days to do your due diligence before signing. To formalise the purchase of a new investment property you'll be asked to enter into one or two contracts.

Contracts by nature are hard to read and full of legal jargon. Have a good read through them regardless to get the general idea, but get yourself straight to a licenced conveyancer upon signing! Check with your licenced conveyancer. If you have the contracts checked by a solicitor / conveyancer first, you waive the cooling off period.

> *#StandEasyTip 1: Here are some basic checks you can consider when you sign the contracts. Complete and check the:*

- full details of the property, including address and lot number
- spelling of your name; and make sure to provide your full name
- correct, full name of your estate agent if you're using one
- correct, full details of legal practitioners or conveyancers that you have engaged
- contracted land price
- deposit amount you'll need to arrange to pay
- inclusion of any special conditions, such as 'subject to finance' clauses.

What does a land contract cover mostly?

Land contracts vary from state to state. Most land contracts cover off details of the offer and acceptance; disclosures; the estate covenants and caveats (building design rules); development approvals and more.

What special conditions or clauses are helpful to have in the contract?

In the first couple of pages on most land contracts you may find a finance clause. It may state that finance is or is not applicable or that the contract may be subject to finance. Subject to finance means that if you signed the contract but your loan request was declined, you can get your deposit back with a letter from the financier.

Most real estate contracts are binding. This means that if you sign the contract you will be bound by law to fulfilling the terms and conditions of the contract.

A wise exit strategy prior to agreeing to the contract is to have a 'subject to finance approval' clause written in, if it isn't already. You don't want to risk losing that hard earned deposit if financing falls through.

What is forward registration and why should I care?

Forward registered land means the land is available for sale even though it hasn't yet been registered with the Land Titles Office. This is because the developer may still be dividing the land into blocks or services such as footpaths, water, power, roads and curbing aren't in yet. Once the land title is gained a building licence is issued and construction can kick off.

This means that as a property investor you can secure a block of land for up to twelve months for a small deposit. This gives you months to get your affairs well in order and secure finance with a lender.

Forward registration is great when the property market is running hot and availability of titled land is low. Vacant land can increase in price between different stage releases.

What does that all mean for you? You can lock the price in today, for a future settlement later.

> *#StandEasyTip 2: If you want to start your property investing career but need three to six months to get money together for settlement, forward registering is a good strategy.*

What do I need to know about a domestic building contract?

Your building contract will include targeted design and finishes for the target tenants – plus the building plans and a detailed list of specifications. Make sure your builder has included all the details of appliance make and models, fittings, fixtures and finishes. Progress payments and warranties will also be detailed in the building contract.

> *#StandEasyTip 3: Agree on a fixed-price lump sum building contract so that there are no surprises for you along the way.*

I also recommend a guaranteed timeline for starting the build, and finishing construction.

> *#StandEasyTip 4: Your building contract is an important pile of paper. It can make a difference between a poor quality build and one that attracts reliable, respectful, good quality tenants.*

It also gives you assurance of no surprises – you know exactly what you're getting for the price upfront. Give it lots of attention, and an expert look over by a legal eagle before you sign.

Don't fall for a cheap marketing hook. Some builders will advertise cheaper construction prices to lure you in. In building you truly do get what you pay for. Cheap construction attracts cheap tenants.

To attract cash flow you need a well-designed, quality (but not over the top with the specifications – no chandeliers and four metre high ceilings!) property that attracts good tenants. If you sell down the track, resale potential will be far greater if build quality is evident.

This is something I overlooked on a deal or two and my returns were affected. Learn from my mistake!

Settlement: a milestone to celebrate!

An exciting milestone for investors is settlement of the land. The timing for settlement will be stated in the contracts. Settlement is time stamped starting with meeting the agreed timeframe for gaining finance.

What you need to stay on top of during the construction phase (a House and Land contract deal)

Celebrate settlement, but do keep in mind that from here on you'll need to pay interest on the land. A swift build is a good build! This interest during the construction phase is tax deductable.

Progress payments are your next priority. These are payments to the builder from your bank or lender to progress each stage of construction.

The first stage in the build contract is the deposit stage. The deposit is paid to the builder to get necessary approvals and make a start.

The second stage and progress payment is the slab or foundations stage. From there you will have three to four progress payments to meet throughout the construction period.

Here is a West Australia example.

The deposit stage is claimed two weeks to two months after (land) settlement, and is 6.5% of the contract price of the build. Slab stage follows and is a 13.5% progress payment, claimed two to three weeks after the deposit stage payment. Then, 20% for brick work is claimed following an additional one to one and a half months after the slab stage. Lock up is the next claim at 40%, and then practical completion. These percentages will vary from contract to contract.

> *#StandEasyTip 5: Stack the cards in your favour by using a fixed price lump sum building contract.*

If the builder hits unforeseen circumstances while building the house, your contract price won't change.

Handover: worthy of a celebration!

Handover is when you officially have a certificate of occupancy, all warranty documentation and the keys to the property handed to you. You will also make your final payment to the builder following a final inspection by you. The pre-handover inspection is your opportunity to audit the building against the contract, and ask for any fixes that aren't up to scratch.

Before hand over you need to have a building inspector in to do the practical building inspection and grant a 'certificate of occupancy' ready for the formal handover.

Once the property is 'handed over,' you need to take over the building insurance from the builder. Building insurance is mandatory with the terms and conditions of your mortgage.

> *#StandEasyTip 6: Landlord insurance is designed to protect you, the investor.*

Finding the right tenants

Employing a good property manager will free up your time and energy for more enjoyable priorities. I would rather be looking for my next property, hanging out with my family, or heading for a surf than chasing up a broken toilet!

A good rental or property manager gives you a buffer between yourself and the tenant. The property manager acts on your behalf with a management agreement in place.

#StandEasyTip 7: Activate your agency agreement a week or two before the property is officially handed over. This means you can line up tenants before handover. Remember, property investment is all about cash flow.

As soon as your tenants have signed the tenancy agreement, your property is ready to claim tax benefits. The trigger is an 'occupant certificate'. From here on, depreciation kicks in. Talk to your accountant about a tax-withholding variation, where your tax breaks can be claimed on a fortnightly basis – cash flow…

While we're on tax benefits the interest accrued in the construction period can be claimed in the coming 30 June tax year.

#StandEasyTip 8: When reviewing potential tenants go for a longer term tenant, ideally a one year or more lease. If you've done your homework well, you'll have a good selection of tenants to pick and choose from.

Over time the vacancy rates may fluctuate. Have the agent do a detailed inspection report if required. To attract new tenants you may need to invest a little in the property to make it more attractive than other properties on the rental market. For example, laying some quality turf to improve a yard or hiring a professional to do a good tidy up could help lift the appeal of your property.

Review

Done properly, property investment is a set and forget strategy but don't ever forget about it! Property markets shift all the time. You need to keep your eye on the market and regularly review your cash flow position - more about that in the next step.

Continue your savings program

Yes you've done well to buy an investment property and get tenants it. Don't stop! Keep up the discipline you have around putting aside cash savings so you can work through from Step 1 again! It'll be much easier the next time around as you'll be learning all the way.

Step 7: Property Investment Review

Keep chipping. Remember this is your trade now. You'll need to continue learning and polishing up to become a skilled property investment tradesperson.

Based on the work you've completed so far you are about to learn more about:

- ◆ Review your property on a regular basis
- ◆ Track property markets
- ◆ Review rental returns every six to twelve months
- ◆ Secure credit at the top of the market
- ◆ Monitor and claim all tax benefits
- ◆ Your ability to review your financial position: a quiz

Review your property on a regular basis

With a professional team supporting you, review your financial position regularly. Investing to the next level requires full awareness of your financial situation.

Here are the factors you'll need to monitor and review for the rest of your investing life:

- State and local property market statistics
- your cash flow
- taxation benefits
- loan and interest rates
- the rental market and vacancy rates
- your property manager.

Track the Australian property markets and local markets

You'll need to get actively involved and review the indicators on a regular basis. Go back to Step 4 for a refresh.

#StandEasyTip 1: It is worthwhile getting a property valuation done once a year.

Most of the top tier banks will do a property valuation for free depending on their current lending policy. Ask your finance broker.

Review rental returns every six to twelve months

First of all make sure that you build a great relationship with your property manager. They are your eyes and ears on the ground. Ask them how the rental market is going at the moment.

Secure credit at the top of the market

A question I'm asked regularly is whether to sell when the property market is at '12 o'clock', at a property cycle peak.

I wouldn't recommend it. An early-in-their-career property investor won't have seen a full property cycle. This means that selling at the first peak, may mean you've not realised the full potential of your property.

In this trade, it is capital you're after. At a 12 o'clock market if you can get a strong valuation of more than thirty percent of equity, you could set up a line of credit, keep your cash flow flowing. Remember that the interest you'll pay on the loan is tax deductable.

In the simplest example, buying an investment property in the 4 o'clock to 8 o'clock property cycle gives the best chances of growth in the initial stages of your investment. In this part of the property clock, the market has bottomed out. The challenge is to time it well. This is what I refer to as the 'Investors Market.'

As with any goal you set, seeing things go well early is a great motivator. Growth in the early days of investing will really kick you along and keep you in the market longer, growing your wealth with more certainty.

#StandEasyTip 2: Signs of an upturn in the market can be:

- vacancy rates contract

- median house or unit prices are increasing

- look for a decrease or low interest rates

- steady to increasing median rent

- increasing sales activity indicated by auction clearance rates and housing and unit sales volumes.

If you buy in the 12 o'clock to 4 o'clock property cycle you'll want to get a discount. Vendors in this market will be dropping their price to get the sale. Buyers are harder to come by and will need to wait through the cycle to gain capital growth. This is what I refer to as the 'Buyers Market.'

The 8 o'clock to 12 o'clock is a buoyant market with high interest from buyers and lots of sales activity. There is a potential to pay too much, be weary in these type markets conditions. I like to refer this as a 'Sellers Market.'

#StandEasyTip 3: Signs of peak market activity can be:

- vacancy rates start to increase

- median house and unit prices start to bounce around.

- look for an increase or higher interest rates.

- declining median rents

- decreasing sales activity indicated by auction clearance rates and housing and unit sales volumes.

History tells us that property cycles can be anywhere from seven to fifteen years from start to finish. Property investing to grow wealth is a long term career choice that rewards patience.

Monitor and claim all tax benefits

Remember, any opportunity to reduce your tax means cash back in your pocket. The key is to get organised and keep all your documentation in one spot and finding a good accountant that gets what you want to achieve.

Keep ship shape records so you don't miss out on tax benefits

Making your accountant or tax agent work through a shoe box of receipts is not making the most of their expertise, and many still charge in 15 minute increments!

Here are some tips for keeping all your investment related documents ship-shape and cash flow friendly:

- **Hit an office supplies store:** invest in an expanding file, or a display book or folder with clear plastic sleeves.

- **Every piece of paper, straight into your file:** receipts and statements are filed as soon as you open them. Make this a non-negotiable to-do.

- **Set up a simple spreadsheet to support your new filing system:** it'll help you get a clear sense of when invoices are due, ahead of time. You'll be able to quickly do some calculations before you visit your accountant. It'll help you focus on asking the right questions, to get the best of your accountant's expert knowledge.

Now you and your accountant can discuss valuable topics such as the latest in tax minimisation strategies. There is a quiz at the end of Step 7 to help you assess how ship shape your record keeping skills are.

A tax depreciation schedule is your new-home-unlocks-cash-flow appreciation schedule!

Quantity Surveyors are recognised by the Australian Taxation Office (ATO) as specialists in preparing tax depreciation schedules for income producing properties. A tax depreciation schedule is your golden ticket to unlocking cash flow. This is why I recommend investing in new builds.

Brand new housing constructions depreciate in value, helping you off-set any losses and saving you thousands of dollars each year in tax deductions.

> *#StandEasyTip 4: Purchasing a new build unlocks tax benefits you simply won't get if you buy an established house that already has already realised depreciation over the years.*

The costs associated with the construction of a new home such as the interest paid during the building period are tax deductable. By settling on your land first, you also minimise stamp duty which is a non tax deductible cost.

Bring a good accountant or tax agent in to your support team

By now you'll have a good understanding of why you need a team of experts to help you reach your financial and lifestyle goals. Head back to Step 3 if you need a refresh on what an expert team looks like.

Hiring professionals is well worth the investment. It will give you confidence that you are in the best possible cash flow position. A best possible cash flow position makes scaling up to two or more properties achievable. An accountant crunches numbers and they understand how to shape them to get the most from them. A good accountant will be happy to hear your ideas, and test them out with calculations.

By learning from experts, you'll find that after your first couple of property deals you'll get a good feel for it. Knowledge is cash in your pocket in a property investing career. You'll get to a point where you can run your own property investment spreadsheet so that you know where you're sitting with your cash at any one point in time.

A property investment spreadsheet includes the numbers on holding costs such as:

- borrowing costs such as bank / lender fees and the interest on your loan
- managing agent associated fees
- water and council rates
- building insurance and landlord insurances
- maximum depreciation from a Quantity Surveyors Report
- tax withholding benefits (once you submit a form with the ATO via your accountant)

Cash flow is king and your accountant, cash flow's loyal subject!

To manage your risk well and so you can sleep soundly each night, you need to find an accountant that has expertise and stays up to date in tax deductions available to property investors. Better still, when you're short listing accountants, ask if they invest in property themselves.

Your goal here is to have expert guidance to help you maximise your cash flow as well as build a cash buffer for unplanned expenses.

The secret is to keep reminding yourself of what you want your future to look like, feel like, smell like and be like. If you need a refresh, grab some pen and paper and head back to Step 1: Setting Goals.

#StandEasyTip 5: A cash buffer is your oxygen when your trade is property investment.

A good rule of thumb is to have at least three months of cash that you can access if you're ever caught short. Even the most experienced of us have had situations arise that we couldn't have planned for. Be a planner, not a punter. You want to rest easy.

Be diligent, keep records, track your goals and get organised.

Keep going!

You've done it. You've taken control by taking the time to educate yourself on the seven steps to successful property investment.

A marathoner or tri-athlete rarely achieves their race pace and next race alone. To achieve great feats, you need a support team and a mentor or two to guide you.

Don't stop at one investment property. Just like getting past the first three kilometres of a marathon, once you've sweated out the first bit, the rest gets easier – if you keep focused on where you're heading to and why. A good mentor will encourage you to talk about your dreams often, help conquer your challenges and help keep you on course.

⚒ : Take a look at Capital Properties' Rental Property Income Tax Return Checklist for a detailed rental property checklist that you can download and use in preparation for end of tax year. Visit capitalproperties.com.au > Resources & Tools > Investor Tools & Apps > Tax Checklist

A Quiz: How ship shape is your record keeping?

1. Give yourself an overall score out of 10 for being organised with your paperwork and softcopy documents (with 10 being 'world class organiser' and 1 being 'I live in complete chaos.')

    #StandEasyTip 1: If you want to achieve success you've got to give one hundred percent.

If you scored yourself less than an 8, its time to shape up!

2. Do you collect all tax deductable bills through the year? These bills include:

*   Water rates (if applicable in your state)
*   Council rates
*   Insurances including landlord insurance and building insurance
*   Rental or Property Manager's fee
*   Maintenance
*   Property inspections (twice a year per property)

    #StandEasyTip 2: Some property investors make the mistake of thinking that capital improvements such as renovations and painting the exterior is tax deductible.

Any expenses related to maintenance work that is deemed by the ATO to improve the capital value does not attract a tax benefit. Repairs and replacements are generally tax deductible.

3. Do you track the bills as they come in, into your property investment spreadsheet?

4. Do you run a property investment worksheet to keep track of your monthly expenditure and incomes?

5. Does your real estate agent schedule in two inspections of your investment property in the first six months after handover?

    #StandEasyTip 3: In the first year of owning a new property, make the most of the defect liability period.

Make sure that either you, or your property manager, go through your property once or twice following hand over.

6. Have you set up a designated bank account to receive rental income and pay the mortgage repayments?

    #StandEasyTip 4: Set up one offset bank account or an account linked with the home loan to separate personal expenditure from your investment income.

It makes it a whole lot easier when it comes to tax time.

7. Do you keep all receipts related to regular visits to your investment property portfolio?

    #StandEasyTip 5: Did you know you can claim a legitimate tax benefit for any expenses associated with inspections?

Schedule in one of your inspections in June each year, just before you lodge your tax returns so you can claim the expense sooner.

8. Do you request updates from property research companies like SQM Research, RP Data and Residex?

    #StandEasyTip 6: Build your own steady supply of well researched property data from companies

like SQM Research, CoreLogic RP Data and Residex so you can start forming your own well educated opinion of where the property market is at, at any one point in time.

9. Do you know what your cash flow is right at this minute?

10. If you have more than one investment property, do you meet with your accountant to do tax planning once per year?

11. Do you use a tax withholding variation to reduce the tax coming out of your salary each fortnight?

12. Do you stay on top of your tax? Do you contact your accountant or tax agent through the year with interest rate or changes to your salary so you don't end up with a tax bill at the end of the year?

13. Are you staying on top of your savings plan of putting away at least 10% of your cash flow?

    #StandEasyTip 7: Always stay one property ahead of your planning.

Think about how a new property purchase might impact future property purchases. You should only be buying properties that allow you to effectively manage your cash flow. You want to have enough cash flow that you can keep with your savings plan to get ready for your next purchase.

How did you rate?

If you answered 'No' to any of the questions above, we need to do some work together. As you gain experience in your new trade, you'll find the better shape your records are in, the easier it is to keep growing!

Send me a #DearMarcus @CapitalProps tweet to let me know how you went, or to ask any questions about reaching your future goals.

: Take a look at Capital Properties' helpful links for property investors and bookmark the URL. Visit capitalproperties.com.au > Resources & Tools > Property Research Tactic.

: Download and save Capital Properties' Rental Property Spreadsheet. Input all your rental statements and any other tax deductible items. You now have a balance sheet ready for your accountant at the end of the financial year. Visit capitalproperties.com.au > Resources & tools > Investor tools & apps > Rental Property Calculator

My reflections for your success

HOW TO RUN A MARATHON ONE FOOT IN FRONT OF THE OTHER

> "We are boxed in the boundary conditions of our thinking." – Albert Einstein

With the right tools, knowledge, support team and proven methods you can bust out of the box. The right mentors and knowledge can propel you toward your best lifestyle.

If you are the smartest person you know in terms of property investing, it is time to find yourself a new team. The network you put around you can be the difference between a mediocre deal and an outcome that gets you to where you want to be sooner.

The synergy of a team cooperating to realise common goals will produce a far superior outcome than an individual can. There is a great story about one ox being able to pull a one tonne load for a farmer, but with a second ox the farmer could have not two, but four tonnes shifted.

The best way to achieve brute strength in moving forward is by bringing on a team of professionals that genuinely understand the challenges of your Defence Force lifestyle, and that care about what you want to achieve.

We know that while you're working with Defence you need a wealth building solution that is:

- understanding to your busy schedule and periods of absence from a routine kind of home life

- low maintenance – while you're learning the ropes you need a professional team that can hold your hand from start to finish – or for as long as you need.

- educational and equips you with proven methodology and knowledge that can help you achieve goals and keep building!

There are real estate agencies that can help you work out a personalised plan targeted to achieve your idea of living well. We can guide and mentor you to apply a time tested, proven strategy that will change the course of your future and leave a legacy for the next generation.

This means you can build an income pipeline while you're managing your job. In some of your spare time, you'll be researching and learning about property to prepare you for your new trade – property investing – getting you ready for your next step. It's that next step that allows you to achieve your idea of your future.

MAKE GOOD CHOICES DRIVEN BY PURPOSE, NOT MONEY

> "Be the chess player, not the chess piece."

You have the choice right now to get in the driver's seat. Put your foot down, drive with confidence and keep the focus on where you're heading.

Build a framework that will support your ideal lifestyle, like I did! If I can do it, you definitely can – you have the added benefit of learning from my experiences.

Embrace the added responsibility that taking control offers you. Set your eyes on your prize. Draw from the discipline of your Defence experience and get the job done.

You're on this planet for a short time. Grab the opportunity while you're young. Retire regret free.

What is your higher purpose? Hint: money is not a driver. Think deeply on your motivations and you'll benefit from the energy that brings. Be a good steward of what's been given to you. If you're reading this SOP, you're in a good place already.

> *"My investments have allowed me to indulge in my surfing when the conditions are calling me. All you need to do is keep it simple. Take one step at a time. Dip your toe in the ocean and get a feel for it. Learn to start reading the swell and how to recognise a rip. It's those rips that can be the easiest way to get out the back and ready for the best ride."*

Fear limits us. Acknowledge that you feel fear. Fear is simply an emotion we feel when what we are really looking for is a solution. Focus on the choices ahead – the solution is right in front of you.

Rise up. You're going to have to push aside the doubters. Doubters are those that perhaps don't have control of their own life but believe that they are protecting your from failure. Back yourself.

I tried many different ways to make money including multi-level marketing, owning vending machines and importing. Choosing the path less travelled to achieve success can attract the detractors' attention. You must be able to rise above this unless it is just an ordinary life – aka Struggle Street- that you are seeking. If someone says you can't do this, make 'life's too short' a standard response. Be extraordinary.

Being in the Defence Force already puts you on a mountain of opportunity in terms of the strategies we've explored in this SOP.

Congratulations for reading this and for being proactive in wanting to take investing to the next level.

You can do this!

Best wishes for what is ahead of you.

Marcus Westnedge

Part 4

Post-script: the next step is your 30 day action plan

We've covered a lot so far. Give yourself a little time to absorb it all, not too much time, and let's go.

Get started

We want you to get this right from the beginning. We'd love to be a part of your team and help you through the steps ahead.

Step 1: Meet with our team

Book in for your free, personalised Discovery Session with the team here and fast track your new trade. You're not committed to anything other than just showing the courtesy of turning up on time – a Defence Force trait you well know.

Register now, while growing wealth is on your mind.

> #StandEasyTip: Make the most of your relationship with your professional support team.

Ask loads of questions. Inquiry is the best way to acquire knowledge. I've learned that you can't be successful solo. Your relationships with your professional support team are the bricks and mortar of the success you can achieve in property investing.

Some of many useful resources and training materials to help you on your way

Before you come in, I have put together some useful resource and training materials to help get you started.

Step 2: Assess your current financial position

Find out exactly where you are financially. Once you complete a budget, you'll know how much you have to put towards investing in your future. If you're not saving money already, start putting aside 10% of your take home pay into a savings account. If you're struggling to find 10%, don't give up. Knowing where you're at is the first step.

Step 3: Set your goals

We've talked in detail about the value of setting clearly defined goals. If you haven't already worked through goal setting earlier on in your reading, now is the time to do it.

⚒ : Book in by completing the registration form at capitalproperties.com.au > Learn & Grow > Free Discovery Session.

⚒ : Complete a Budget Spreadsheet. You'll find a template at capitalproperties.com.au > Investor Tools & Apps > Resources & Tools > Investor Tools & Apps > Budget Planner.

⚒ : Complete a Goal Setting Workbook. You'll find this at capitalproperties.com.au > Investor Tools & Apps > Goal Setting Worksheet

Free presentations and workshops ready for the willing

Take the opportunity right in front of you. Educate yourself by registering to attend one of our free events facilitated by experienced portfolio builders.

Step 4: Educate yourself

We are growing our Switched-on Property Investors (SPI) Program for Defence people and friends. It's free to join and we'll keep you up to date with regular email newsletters and VIP invitations to events.

Make informed investment choices by understanding the numbers that count. Our free online calculators, spreadsheets and checklists will help you make well informed decisions from setting goals to helping prepare your rental property tax income return.

Step 5: Surround yourself with people sharing property investment goals

Join a like minded community of Defence investors where you can exchange ideas and keep your information fresh and vibrant.

MY CHALLENGE TO THE DEFENCE FORCE PROPERTY INVESTOR TRADIE

My team and I at Capital Properties believe that Defence Force investors that serve at least six years can invest in three investment properties within that time frame.

Everything I've laid out in this SOP has been directly linked to this belief in your opportunity.

Imagine walking from service after a six year stint of serving your country, with a million dollar plus property portfolio?

We've helped over a thousand military families achieve their goals in real estate and we can do the same for you.

We get the military lifestyle. We know how time consuming and overwhelming the job can get at times and that trying to succeed in something like property investment that 'ain't part of ship' can be daunting.

✗ : Join our SPI Program by registering your details at capitalproperties.com.au > Learn & Grow > Join our SPI Program
Check in to our free property investment workshops, presentations and events for Defence Force property investors. Go to capitalproperties.com.au > Learn & Grow > Upcoming events

✗ : Explore all the free tools and resources available to you at capitalproperties.com.au > Tools & Resources > Investor tools & apps

✗ : Join in the conversations on our Facebook page. Go to Facebook.com/CapitalPropertiesHQ. Find out about our Defence Force 3 properties in 6 years challenge by registering to attend our free one hour Discovery Session. Complete the registration form at capitalproperties.com. au > Learn & Grow > Free Discovery Session. Who dares, wins!

Trust is the other challenge. Who can you trust? It often feels like everyone is after a slice of your salary with promises.

Capital Properties offers a complete support system, holding your hand through the whole investment process while acknowledging that a posting away from home presents a unique set of challenges.

Educating you so you can learn how to sustain the path to reaching your lifestyle goals is a priority for us at Capital Properties.

Being ex-military means that the team I lead understand the importance of tailoring plans to suit Defence lifestyles.

Many of our clients are Navy Engineers, Electronic Technicians and Clearance Divers in their 20s who have been in service for a year or two. They share a common goal of wanting to accumulate assets while they're in service.

This program is for the proactive member who wants a flying start - a proactive member who wants some assistance with future planning and discovering future goals. This program is best suited to those that take action to get stuff done and that recognise they need to do something smart with some of their pay. If you're open to fresh ideas and to give your future a decent crack, we'd love to work with you.

Who are you?

You'll fall into one of two categories:

- you enjoy your Defence job and you're looking at staying put for a longer period of time; or,
- the Defence Force is okay but it is a springboard for getting your qualifications to move into another industry.

Regardless of which category you fall in to, imagine having a couple of property assets by the time you leave. You're better off with assets, than without them!

Get a taste of what it is like to be a Defence Property Investor by joining our Switched-on Property Investors (SPI) program. You'll find the details on our website, or earlier in this section.

Aim for 3 property investments in 6 years. We dare you!

To set yourself up over your 6 year Defence career and leave with 3 property assets, you need to meet the following criteria for success. You must:

- have a minimum income of $60,000 per year, base salary
- start with $40,000 in savings
- be able to save at least $12,000 per year
- pass the minimum finance requirement
- have a clear credit history and pass the credit history test.
- minimal personal debts

All service men and women have a phenomenal opportunity to secure their and their families', financial futures.

All success takes is a shift in thinking

Welcome our team as your mentors and guides and we'll leave you feeling like you are educated on what you are doing. You'll gain so much from the experience that you'll want to repeat the process to leave an ongoing legacy.

Step 1: Know where you want to be in the future

We will delve deep into your short, medium and long term goals. For a refresher on the value of goal setting, revisit the beginning of this SOP *Step 1: Set financial goals to successfully reach your future goals.*

Step 2: Know where you are financially

Sit down and review your finances at our free Discovery Session with one of our expert team members by filling in a self-evaluation, together. You'll learn where you are right now and how much you can put toward investing in your future. We'll break it down for you into a per week amount so you can really picture what it means.

Step 3: Book in to your free Discovery Session now

This session gives us an opportunity to explore the possibility of working together. Our 7 step process to successfully invest in property isn't for everyone. You'll meet with a Capital Properties' Investment Director who will explain how we operate and what we do.

Step 4: Join our Pinnacle Support Program

Our Pinnacle Support Program keeps going as long as you need us.

You now have at least one property bringing you rental returns, growing equity and giving you cash flow to fund your next investment. We want you to keep reaching toward your next pinnacle.

Being a switched-on property investor, you'll know that investing in real estate isn't a set and forget strategy. Growing a property portfolio to fund your lifestyle goals (and give your parents bragging rights...) requires regular review of your financial position and investment artillery.

We know your Defence lifestyle doesn't leave you with spare wriggle room to crunch numbers, coordinate property valuations, review rental returns and bring the next part of your growth strategy to life. We can help.

The question many first-time investors ask is, "...when should I purchase an investment property?"

My mentor would say, "...when you can". As your mentor I say - let's get started!

⚒ : Book in by completing the registration form at capitalproperties.com.au > Learn & Grow > Free Discovery Session.

⚒ : Find out more about our Pinnacle Program at capitalproperties.com.au > Invest & Grow > Pinnacle Support Program.

WHAT ARE OUR CLIENTS SAYING ABOUT US?

When you're young and mobile – or young in outlook – scraping off some of your Defence pay to invest can feel like a commitment you're not ready to make.

Once you take the first step, work with us to set some goals, crunch some numbers and buy that first property, you'll catch the infectious Property Investment Bug (affectionately known as the PIB}.

The earlier the PIB sets in, the easier it is to buy your next property and grow a self-sustaining income.

Some of your peers are already there. Here are some sound bites from Defence people that were once like you.

⚒ : Read testimonials from people that were once like you. Go to capitalproperties.com.au > About > Testimonials

facebook.com > CapitalpropertiesHQ > Review

Appendix: property investment calculations explained

In Step 2: Access your resources I referred to some key factors that a loan or mortgage broker will take into consideration. Here is a summary of some of the calculations you'll get to know as you hone your property investment trade.

WHAT IS EQUITY?

Equity is the difference between the bank or lender's valuation of your property, and the debt that you owe on it.

WHAT DOES LOAN TO VALUE RATIO (LVR) MEAN?

Your LVR is the amount you are borrowing as a percentage of the value of the property you're using as security for the loan. For example a 95% LVR means you are handing over a 5% deposit to your lender. A 5% deposit plus enough money to cover all your fees is all you need to get started in most cases. The additional fees equates to roughly 5% of the value of the property – a combined total of 10% of the purchase price of the property.

For example, a property priced at $400,000 may require you to take out a loan of $320,000 (80% of the purchase price). This is an 80% LVR. That means, you need to put down a $80,000 deposit (20% of the purchase price of the property).

If you have a property portfolio valued at $1 million (well done!), the total loan could be $800,000 (80% of the value of the property – an 80% LVR) where the equity position is $200,000.

The LVR is important because banks will view you differently to the next person in terms of the size of deposit to put down and the amount of debt you have. This goes the same for the property you are looking to purchase. It all depends on the banking policies at the time of purchase. Lenders policies s change regularly.

WHAT IS AN ASSESSMENT RATE?

The Assessment Rate is the higher interest rate the bank uses to calculate your ability to service debt to make sure you can afford the lending and manage through fluctuations in interest rates.

WHAT DOES DEBT TO SERVICE RATIO (DSR) MEAN?

The other key factor lenders look at is debt servicing. Contact your mortgage broker to get a more detailed breakdown on your DSR. In simple terms, lenders will crunch numbers based on your total debts and will calculate the interest payable on a higher interest rate - the assessment rate.

Here is a high level example. With a total of $300,000 of debt owing to the lender on your investment portfolio, if you wanted to borrow a further $300,000 here is how you would calculate your DSR. Your total borrowings are calculated at $600,000 that needs to be repaid at an 8%* assessment rate. *The assessment rate can change please use this as a guide only. This calculates to $48,000 of interest only (IO).

Your total income is then calculated by summing your PAYG income plus rental incomes. If you were earning $100,000 per year and receiving rental incomes of $300 per week, your total income would calculate as follows:

PAYG income = $100,000

Rental income = [$300 x 52]*80% = $24, 960

Total income is $100,000 + $24,960 = $125,000 (rounding up)

Interest only = $48,000

DSR is [loan repayments or in this case IO amount] / total income * 100:

$48,000 (IO) / $125,000 * 100 = 38.4%

As a general rule banks and lenders' sweet spot for debt servicing is 30 to 35% and sometimes as high as 40%.

These calculations are just working examples to give you a rough idea of where you might be sitting. Get the 'good oil' from your professional mortgage broker.

#StandEasyTip 1: It's good practice to do a financial health check on a biannual or quarterly basis.

The reason for this is to optimise your position favourably to gain finance.

#StandEasyTip 2: Get your broker to do the leg work when it comes to applying for a mortgage.

Good finance brokers know how to present your current situation to the bank for the best chance of getting approval.

#StandEasyTip 3: If you're not ready just yet, reposition yourself and try again.

A good investor is always looking to do a deal. If there's still no joy, get some help and pinpoint where your funds are going, and track your spend through a budget spending worksheet like this one – download our budget spending worksheet at:

capitalproperties.com.au > Resources & Tools > Investor Tools & Apps > Budget Planner

If you are ready to go, identify an asset to suit your borrowing capacity and your investment goals.

WHAT IS LENDERS MORTGAGE INSURANCE (LMI)?

Staying with the theme of keeping it simple, LMI is an insurance premium that will cover the bank's losses if you default on your loan. If the bank was to repossess your property and doesn't make its money back by selling it, the insurance company makes up the shortfall for the bank. LMI is not like a get-out-of-jail-free card! If the insurer ends up out of pocket, it will come after the money eventually.

LMI is payable on loans with an 80% loan-to-value ratio (LVR) or greater. Some investors that we meet fret about paying the LMI premium. No need to fret! LMI is tax deductable two-fold – firstly over 5 years, as part of your set up costs. Then, the interest accrued when capitalised is also tax deductable helping you get into the market sooner rather than later.

If you've got a long timeline in property the best scenario is using as little of your own money as possible, and more of the bank's money.

This can be achieved by putting down a 5% deposit and 95% LVR, capitalising as much as possible of the LMI onto the loan.

: You'll find a number of LMI Calculators online. We like using this one at genworth.com. au > Online tools, forms and reports > LMI Premium Estimator

WHICH WAY TO GO: AN INTEREST ONLY OR A PRINCIPLE AND INTEREST LOAN?

The real question here is do you want manageable cash flow?

Interest only loans frees up cash flow to help you maintain a property to keep your savings going to build a portfolio. Of course, the principle will still need to be paid down later when you need the cash flow.

Your best strategy when you're young is to accumulate assets first, then reduce debt and increase cash flow in your retirement.

Another way to look at it is why would you use tax paid money to pay down a tax deductable debt? It's counterintuitive!

HERE IS AN EXAMPLE OF WHAT A 5% DEPOSIT AND COSTS COULD LOOK LIKE

Purchase price $400,000

Land $180,000

Build $220,000

Deposit and costs

5% deposit $20,000

Stamp duty   *$4,500

Solicitors fees $1,500

Bank fees $1,500

Miscellaneous fees $1,000

Total Deposit and Costs **$28,500

* Stamp Duty based on the land only. Costs may vary from state to state.

** This amount is a guide only. Costs may vary from state to state.

Printed in the United States
By Bookmasters